THE GOURD BOOK

by
CHARLES B. HEISER, JR.

WITHDRAWN

University of Oklahoma Press : Norman and London

By Charles B. Heiser, Jr.

Nightshades: The Paradoxical Plants (San Francisco, 1969)
Seed to Civilization: The Story of Man's Food (San Francisco, 1973)
The Sunflower (Norman, 1976)
The Gourd Book (Norman, 1979)
Of Plants and People (Norman, 1985)

To Jack Humbles
and T. W. Whitaker
who started me
on a study of gourds

Library of Congress Cataloging in Publication Data

Heiser, Charles Bixler, 1920–
    The gourd book.

    Bibliography: p. 235
    Includes index.
    1. Gourds. I. Title
SB317.G68H44   635'.62   78–21389
ISBN: 0–8061–1524–6 (cloth)
ISBN: 0–8061–2572–1 (paper)

2   3   4   5   6   7   8   9   10   11

89495

Contents

Preface to the Paperback Edition

Although I have had little opportunity to grow gourds for the past several years, my interest in them continues. By way of this new preface I should like to mention recent developments with gourds that I have found of particular interest.

At the time this book was written it was not known if the Texas gourd was an escape from cultivation or an indigenous plant. Since that time, chiefly through the work of Deena Decker-Walters, [1]* it appears that it is the latter, and moreover that the Texas gourd is the progenitor of the squash (*Cucurbita pepo*) in eastern North America. It previously had been thought that this squash had originated in Mexico and been carried northward. Now it seems likely that the squash had separate origins in Mexico and eastern North America.

It generally has been thought that the bottle gourd was carried by people from Mexico to eastern North America, although there was a possibility that it arrived naturally by ocean drift. If the latter did occur, Florida was the most likely place for its arrival. It is therefore of considerable interest that the oldest gourd known north of Mexico, over 7,000 years old, has been reported from a site in east-central Florida. [2] Although this discovery, of course, does not prove that the gourd first reached Florida by ocean drift, I feel that it strengthens the possibility that it did so. The squash and the bottle gourd are among the oldest cultivated plants in eastern North America and along with the sunflower and other native species were in cultivation before corn and other plants arrived from Mexico.

A few years ago the hedgehog gourd was an obscure plant, but it has now become well known under the name kiwano. I first saw the fruits in our markets in 1986, and after trying them I concluded that they were more objects of curiosity and conver-

*Numbers refer to numbered entries in References, page vi.

sation than for eating. To my surprise they still appear in our vegetable markets, but I predict that as a food plant they will soon disappear. Julia Morton [7] has provided us with an excellent account of the plant.

Until recently only one species of the loofah gourd was known to be native to the Americas. Additional study has shown that there are three indigenous species, one in Middle America and two in northern South America. [1] It has also been shown that some species of *Luffa* have fruits that will float in salt water for several months and still retain some seed viability. Correct names of the American loofahs can be found in Jeffrey. [5]

A few years ago I saw an item in the newspaper about a new medicine, trichosanthin, from China. With that name it was obvious that it was derived from the genus *Trichosanthes*, to which the snake gourd belongs. Eventually I learned [6] that the medicine came from the species *Trichosanthes kirilowii*. Moreover, I found that it was not a new drug, but an ancient one used in China for abortion and the treatment of certain kinds of cancer.

The supposed contamination of squashes by the pollen of gourds is briefly discussed in the book. A more detailed treatment will be found in my more recent book. [4]

Although I was aware that the bottle gourd played a role in Chinese mythology, I had no idea how prominent that role was until I read the book by Girardot. [3]

Other news of gourds, particularly relating to gourdcraft, will be found in *The Gourd*, the publication of the American Gourd Society, Inc. (P. O. Box 274, Mt. Gilead, Ohio 43338). The spring 1992 number has a listing of all of the articles that have appeared in the last twenty-one volumes. Unfortunately, I have been able to attend their gourd show only twice in the last ten years. However, from these visits as well as from reports of friends who attend annually, I can say that the show gets bigger and better every year. I should also like to take this opportunity to credit a member of the gourd society, Mrs. Walter Rinehart, for her prize-winning exhibit, a photo of which appears among the color plates. She also made one of the bird houses (p. 139). I would also like to extend thanks to those people who have written letters to me about gourds, in particular Theo Shoon of New Zealand, who is an authority on gourds and was instrumental in reviving interest in gourds among the Maori.

Charles B. Heiser, Jr.

Bloomington, Indiana

References

1. D. M. Bates, R. W. Robinson, and C. Jeffrey, *Biology and Utilization of the Cucurbitaceae* (Ithaca, New York, Cornell University Press, 1990).
2. Glen H. Doran, D. N. Dickel, and L. A. Newsom, "A 7,290-year-old bottle gourd from the Windover Site, Florida," *American Antiquity* 55, 354–60 (1990).
3. H. J. Girardot, *Myth and Meaning in Early Taoism* (Berkeley, University of California Press, 1983).
4. C. Heiser, *Of Plants and People* (Norman, University of Oklahoma Press, 1985).
5. C. Jeffrey, "The application of names to the indigenous neotropical species of *Luffa* Mill. (Cucurbitaceae)," *Kew Bulletin* 47, 471–72 (1992).
6. J. M. Maraganore, M. Joseph, and M. C. Bailey, "Purification and characterization of trichosanthin," *Journal of Biological Chemistry* 262, 11628–33 (1987).
7. Julia Morton, "The horned cucumber, alias 'Kiwano' (*Cucumis metuliferus*, Cucurbitaceae)," *Economic Botany* 4, 325–27 (1987).

Preface to the First Edition

Why a book on gourds? The answer is very simple: I felt like writing such a book. I have enjoyed growing gourds for a number of years, I have done research on some of them, and I think that there are many people who will enjoy learning more about them. In addition to being ornamental, they have been of considerable service to mankind. Although never more than minor food plants, some of them became most important to man as utensils. There is evidence that a gourd was among man's earliest cultivated plants. In fact, it has even been postulated that it may have been his first cultivated plant. This book is not intended as a scientific monograph, but I hope it will prove to be both accurate and useful. More than that, I hope that it may stimulate someone to undertake scientific investigation of the many problems yet unstudied in gourds.

There is also a second reason for writing this book. After I had completed the writing of my last book (on sunflowers), my colleague and friend Richard Starr said to me, "Well, this is it. You now have written up everything that you know!" I had to prove him wrong.

It is impossible for me to name all of the people who have been of assistance in one way or another in the preparation of this book, and I shall single out but a few. My wife, Dorothy, and Virginia Flack have read the manuscript and offered many helpful suggestions, some of which I have accepted. Carol Daugherty has translated various French works for me. Many individuals and organizations have provided photographs, and with one exception they are named with their photographs. The one exception is for the illustration on page 144. This photograph to the best of my knowledge was sent to me around 1968, but somehow it got separated from the letter accompanying it, and although I have since made considerable effort to learn the source I have been unable to do so. To this individual I send my special thanks and apologies. Most of the photographs of gourds in displays were taken by me at the Ohio Gourd Show in 1975, and I thank the many members of the Gourd Society for their splendid cooperation. Kathleen O'Connell has done the drawings. There remain the many individuals who have supplied me seeds, most of whom have been acknowledged in my earlier papers. To all of these people I extend my thanks.

The title of this book can hardly be said to be very original but it is descriptive. I considered calling the book "Out of My Gourd," and perhaps my readers may decide that this would have been a better title.

Charles B. Heiser, Jr.

Bloomington, Indiana

PART I
MISCELLANEOUS GOURDS

1.
Introduction

Although I expect that most people who read this book will have a pretty good idea as to what a gourd is, I shall begin by trying to define "gourd" as well as "calabash." This is not as easy as one might think.

According to the *Oxford English Dictionary*, the word in its first sense is used for the large fleshy fruit of trailing or climbing plants of the botanical family Cucurbitaceae, and specifically for the fruit of the bottle gourd. The word first appeared as "gourdys" in 1303, as "goordis" in 1382, and around 1440 in the *Promptorium Parvulorum*, the first English-Latin dictionary, we find "goorde" translated as "cucumber . . . cucurbita . . . coloquintida." Although the word *gourd* today is used in England to include the pumpkins and squashes, this could not have been so in the fourteenth century, for squashes and pumpkins had not yet reached Europe from the Americas. By 1555 we find one writer speaking of "melones, gourdes, cucumbers, and such other," so apparently several plants were being called "gourd" by that time. This may well have included the bottle gourd, which was fairly well known in Europe by then. The bottle gourd was grown in England before 1597, for the herbalist John Gerard's description leaves no doubt as to the plant he called "gourd." In 1624, Capt. John Smith wrote that the "chief instruments or Rattles" of the Virginia Indians were made of "small gourds or Pumpeon shells," almost certainly a reference to the bottle gourd.

Words may change their meaning with the passage of time, and for most of us it makes little difference how the word *gourd* was once used. So we can leave the origin of *gourd* and its changing meanings to others and turn to modern usage. The American botanist and authority on cultivated plants L. H. Bailey in his book *Garden of Gourds*, 1937, pointed out that in common language in North America a gourd is a hard-shelled durable fruit grown for ornament, utensils, and general interest. This is the definition that I shall accept. Bailey included several "gourds" in his book that do not meet his definition, and I shall likewise do so.

Bailey limited his gourds to the family Cucurbitaceae. There is one plant, however, that does not belong to this family but meets his definition of a gourd. This is the calabash tree, or tree gourd, native to tropical America. One might perhaps use the word *calabash* for the fruit of this tree and reserve the word *gourd* for the fruit of certain cucurbits, but the words cannot be separated so readily. "Calabash," *calabaza* in Spanish, *calebasse* in French, is probably from a Persian word meaning "melon." The word *calabash* is often used for the fruit of the American tree, but in Africa it has long been applied to the fruit of the bottle gourd, an entirely different plant. In fact, the two words were early regarded as synonymous, for in 1596 we find Sir Walter Raleigh calling "for his calabaza or gourds. . . ." Today it seems hopeless to try to make any distinction between "calabash" and "gourd."

By now it should have become apparent that common names of plants can be very ambiguous and that we need names that are precise. Such precision is provided by scientific names, for although a plant may have many common names it can have only one scientific name. An explanation of taxonomic categories and of the cucurbit family will help

4

clear up some of the confusion that may have been introduced in the previous paragraphs.

The basic unit of classification is the species. As a rule, a species has several characteristics that distinguish it from other species. Its distinctness is preserved because all members of a species are able to interbreed freely, but they will not cross readily with other species. However, by no means is a species uniform in all of its characters, as is quite apparent in the human species. We shall also find that most species of gourds are quite variable in some of their characteristics, particularly those that relate to the size, shape, and color of the fruit. A group of related species makes up a genus (plural, genera). A genus, like a species, also generally shares certain features in common that separate it from other genera. A group of related genera, in turn, makes up a family. There are over three hundred families of flowering plants. The family of greatest concern to us here is the Cucurbitaceae, for all but one of the gourds belong to this family.

The cucurbit family comprises over one hundred genera and less than a thousand species, most of which are tropical. These plants may be characterized as follows: mostly tendril-bearing vines; leaves alternately arranged on the stem, usually five-lobed or divided; flowers usually unisexual, male (staminate) and female (pistillate) borne on the same plant, or sometimes on separate plants; sepals, five; corolla of five petals, separate to the base or united; stamens, five, or sometimes fewer, anthers frequently somewhat fused; ovary inferior, that is, borne below the sepals and petals, becoming a fruit with a soft or hard (as in the true gourds) outer covering and usually containing many seeds attached in three places on the outer wall. Botanically speaking, the fruit is a special type of berry known as a *pepo*. (If any of the foregoing terms are unfamiliar, they may be found in any good dictionary.)

Many of the characteristics listed above are also found in other families, but in combination they serve to distinguish the Cucurbitaceae from all other families of plants.

Members of the family are not very common in the wild

Key

Trees	1.	*Tree Gourd*
Vines		
Petals white		
Petals not fringed		
Petals generally over 1 1/2 in. long; fruit green to white and hard at maturity	2.	*Bottle gourd*
Petals generally less than 1 1/2 in. long; fruit usually tuberculate, orange, and split open at maturity	7.	*Bitter gourd*
Petals fringed	6.	*Snake gourd*
Petals lemon yellow to orange		
Fruits bristly or spiny at maturity		
Fruits bristly or burlike	8.	*Teasel gourd*
Fruits spiny or tuberculate		
Flower stalk bearing a shield-like bract; fruit hollow	7.	*Bitter gourd*
Flower stalk without shield-like bract; fruit solid	9.	*Hedgehog gourd*
Fruits smooth, ridged, warty, or hairy at maturity		
Males flowers borne several to a stalk; fruit with a dry papery rind and fibrous interior	4.	*Loofah gourd*
Male flowers generally one to a stalk; fruit not as above		
Petals separate to base; sepals somewhat leafy and strongly reflexed; fruit hairy when young, covered with wax at maturity	5.	*Wax gourd*
Petals united for nearly half or more of their length; sepals not particularly leafy; fruit durable or perishable, but not strongly hairy or waxy	3.	*Cucurbita gourds*

in the United States (with the exception of the buffalo gourd in the Southwest), but some of them are very familiar in cultivation. They include pumpkins and squashes, various species of the genus *Cucurbita;* the watermelon, *Citrullus vulgaris;* and the cucumber and muskmelon, different species of *Cucumis.*

One does not have to know the characters of the family to grow and enjoy gourds, of course, but such knowledge might increase one's enjoyment. It also might be practical, as in the case of the new gardener who was puzzled because his squash plant (it could well have been a gourd) was producing many flowers but few fruits. So he asked his neighbor, who happened to be a biochemist affiliated with the botany department of a nearby university, what was wrong with his plants. The biochemist thought about it and finally said that perhaps his plant needed more fertilizer. The next day at a staff meeting the biochemist happened to mention his neighbor's problem, whereupon the taxonomist gently informed him that squash plants have separate male and female flowers; and one could hardly expect the former to produce fruits. In fact, a plant will usually bear far more male flowers than it does female; and often times it may produce several male flowers before any female flowers appear.

To introduce the gourds—both the true gourds and most of the other plants that are commonly called gourds—I present the key on page 6. The key gives two choices, and if one has a plant at hand he may, by making the correct choices, identify it. But if the key doesn't serve that purpose, one shouldn't be overly concerned, for it should still be possible to identify the plant by means of the descriptions and illustrations to be given in other chapters of this book.

1. The calabash tree, or tree gourd, *Crescentia cujete,* native to tropical America, belongs to the family Bignoniaceae. This family includes the catalpa tree and the trumpet creeper, both better known in the United States than the tree gourd. It also includes the tropical sausage tree, *Kigelia pinnata,* which has somewhat gourd-

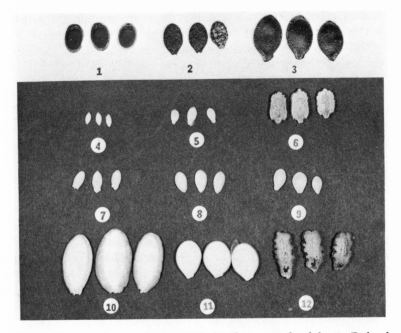

Seeds of various gourds ($\times$ 2/3). 1, Common loofah; 2, Ridged loofah; 3, Fig-leaf; 4, Teasel; 5, Hedgehog; 6, Bitter; 7, Wax; 8, Buffalo; 9, Ornamental; 10, Silver-seed; 11, Turban; 12, Snake.

like fruits, one to one and a half feet long, hanging on long stalks. The tree gourd has fruits that are used for utensils, musical instruments, and for decoration, much the same way as the bottle gourd is used. (Chapter 2.)

2. The bottle gourd, *Lagenaria siceraria*, is apparently native to Africa but had spread to both Asia and the Americas in prehistoric times. How it reached America from Africa is still an unsolved problem. Its large durable fruits have made it extremely useful to man, and it is the plant that is most often meant when the name *gourd* is used. It will be the subject of the last half of this book.

3. The genus *Cucurbita* contains several species that are of interest. First, there are the several wild species in the Americas, whose small fruits can be classed as gourds. One of these, the

buffalo gourd, *Cucurbita foetidissima,* a common plant in the southwestern United States, receives some treatment in a later chapter. There are five cultivated species, which include our familiar squashes and pumpkins. The squashes and pumpkins do not belong to any single species. In fact, these common names have no precise botanical meaning, and there is no real distinction between a squash and a pumpkin. Four of these cultivated species also include plants called gourds. These are the ornamental gourds belonging to *Cucurbita pepo;* the Malabar or fig-leaf gourd, *C. ficifolia;* the silver-seed gourd, *C. mixta;* and the turban gourds, *C. maxima.* Of these only the ornamental gourds can be considered true gourds, but all of them will be treated here in due time. (Chapter 4.)

All of the other gourds given in the key might be called false gourds, because their fruits do not meet the definition of true gourds. But inasmuch as the name *gourd* seems strongly attached to them, they are included in this book.

4. The loofah gourds *(Luffa aegyptiaca* and *L. acutangula),* both native to tropical Asia, are grown for the fibrous interior of their fruits, which are widely used as sponges as well as in other ways. (Chapter 5.)

5. The wax gourd, *Benincasa hispida,* also from tropical Asia, is grown primarily as a food plant and is particularly important in the Orient. The fruit reaches lengths of sixteen inches and is covered with a white wax at maturity. Although the fruits may not be true gourds, I have known some to last longer than two years. (Chapter 6.)

6. The snake gourd *(Trichosanthes cucumerina),* primarily a food plant in India and southeastern Asia, is sometimes grown for its curious fruits, which may be quite slender and reach lengths of six feet. It is also well worth growing for its delicately fringed, fragrant flowers. (Chapter 6.)

7. The bitter gourd, *Momordica charantia,* is perhaps better known as the "balsam pear." It is native to the Old World tropics, but today it is fairly widely grown in the Americas as a food or medicinal plant or as an ornamental for its curious fruit and rather attractive foliage. The name *bitter gourd* is also sometimes used for other gourds. (Chapter 6.)

8. and 9. The teasel gourd, *Cucumis dipsaceus*, and the hedgehog gourd, *Cucumis metuliferus*, will be treated together, for they belong to the same genus. Both are native to Africa and are grown in this country solely for their curious fruits. (Chapter 6.)

There are still other plants called gourd—for example, the fluted gourd, *Telfairia occidentalis*, the ivy gourd, *Coccinia indica*, and the round gourd, *Praecitrullus fistulosus*—that are rather poorly known and so far as I know are not grown in the United States. They will not be treated in this book. There is one gourd that is not grown in the United States, however, that will be included. As anyone familiar with the Bible knows, gourds are mentioned in connection with Jonah and Elisha. Exactly what plants are meant is far from certain, but they will make a good place to start our account.

2.
Gourds of the Bible

And the Lord God prepared a gourd, and made it to come up over Jonah, that it might be a shadow over his head, to deliver him from his grief. So Jonah was exceeding glad of the gourd. Jonah 4:6.

There are great difficulties in trying to identify precisely the plants mentioned in the Bible. Most recent authorities, however, agree that Jonah's "gourd" is not a gourd at all, nor even a member of the family Cucurbitaceae, but rather the castor-bean plant. In some versions of the Bible, Palma Christi, which is a name for the castor bean, is given instead of gourd. The castor bean is a rapid grower, reaching heights of fifteen feet or more in a single season, and has rather large leaves, so it could qualify as a good shade plant. Some earlier writers on the subject did maintain that Jonah's plant was a gourd, one claiming that it was the ornamental gourd (Cucurbita pepo var. ovifera). This gourd, however, was not known in the Old World until after the discovery of America, which certainly eliminates it from consideration. If Jonah's gourd were a true gourd, the most likely candidate would be the bottle gourd, which was known in Egypt around 2000 B.C. Some modern translators of the Bible avoid all the difficulties by changing "gourd" to "plant."

And one went out into the field to gather herbs, and found a wild vine, and gathered thereof wild gourds his lap full, and came and shred them into the pot of pottage: for they knew them not. So they

11

Jonah's "gourd"—the castor bean.

poured out for the men to eat. And it came to pass, as they were eating of the pottage, that they cried out, and said, O thou man of God, there is death in the pot. And they could not eat thereof. 2 Kings 4:39–40.

There does seem to be agreement that the gourd in 2 Kings, or Elisha's gourd, is the *colocynth*, sometimes called the *bitter* or *wild gourd*, *Citrullus colocynthis*. It is a member of the cucurbit family and belongs to the same genus as the watermelon. The plant is found in western Asia, parts of the Mediterranean area, and Africa. It is a vine with yellow flowers and gourdlike fruits about the size and shape of a small orange. The fruits contain a soft pulp that is exceed-

Elisha's gourd—the colocynth, or bitter gourd. Upper left, male
flower; upper right, female flower. (Redrawn from Baillon.)

13

ingly bitter and poisonous. It was formerly widely used as a purgative and still has use in medicine as a drug. It is also reported that the fruits are used for keeping moths out of clothing and that the root was used in northern Rhodesia "for homicidal purposes." Arabs have used the pulverized fruit in the preparation of gunpowder, tinder, and fuses. The seeds are not ordinarily eaten, but after long boiling to remove the poison they have been used for food. Donkeys are said to be the only animals to eat the fruits, but some other animals may graze on the leaves. It is not unlikely that the fruit on sight might be mistaken for an edible melon, but one taste would erase any doubt. It is also considered by some who have written on the subject that "gall" in the Old Testament, usually referred to in connection with wormwood as "symbolic of bitter calamity," is the colocynth. The "vine of Sodom" may also be this plant.

And the cedar of the house within was carved with knops and open flowers. . . . 1 Kings 6:18.

And under the brim of it round about there were knops compassing it, ten in a cubit, compassing the sea round about: the knops were cast in two rows, when it was cast. 1 Kings 7:24.

Some modern translations of the Bible give "gourds" for the "knops" of the King James Version, but exactly what plant, if indeed it was even a plant, Solomon used to decorate the temple must remain a mystery.

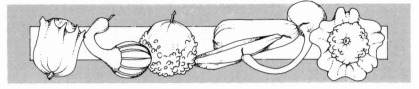

3.
Tree Gourds

In many accounts of the gourds, or calabashes, of tropical America, it is often difficult, if not impossible, to determine whether the writer is referring to the tree gourd or the bottle gourd. This is not surprising, for the same name may be used for both, and the fruits are used in similar ways.

The plants that bear the two gourds are quite different, however, and anyone who has seen the calabash tree is not likely to forget it. Even botanists who are familiar with the great diversity of plants have referred to this tree loaded with its green, pumpkinlike fruits as an almost unbelievable sight. Even without fruit, the long, nearly horizontal branches with leaves clustered at intervals give the tree a distinctive appearance.

Although usually a small tree, it may reach heights of forty feet. The short-stalked flowers have a tubular corolla, about two inches long, and are yellowish or pale green with streaks of purple. They are reported to be pollinated by bats. But it is the fruit that is of greatest interest here. Those of wild plants are often no larger than baseballs, but in cultivation the globular, oval, or oblong fruits may reach lengths of nearly eighteen inches and be a foot wide. The hard outer

15

Tree gourd in Tena, Ecuador.

rind encloses a white pulp in which the seeds are embedded.

The tree grows naturally in hot, somewhat arid regions, although it can be cultivated in the wet tropics. It ranges from Mexico and the West Indies to Brazil and Peru, and its extensive distribution is probably due in no small measure to man's carrying the plant from place to place. Whether it was originally native to Middle America or to South America is not clear. It does apparently occur as a wild plant in Middle America, and I am inclined to think that it was carried from there to South America and the West Indies in prehistoric times. The plant has more recently been introduced to other areas and has been cultivated in south Florida. How the plant spreads naturally is not entirely understood. The fruits have been reported in beach drift in the West Indies and as

16

far away as the Scandinavian Islands. In all the fruits examined from drifts the seeds have been dead. This does not eliminate the possibility, however, that short-distance dispersal occurs by water. Inasmuch as the plant apparently thrives best in savannahlike areas, water can hardly be thought of as a particularly effective agent for dispersal. I shall have more to say about our lack of knowledge concerning dispersal of gourds in other places. The subject deserves more investigation.

Scientifically the plant is known as *Crescentia cujete*, the name having been given it by the great Swedish naturalist, Linnaeus. He chose the genus name to commemorate Pietro de Crescenzi, a thirteenth-century Italian writer on horticulture and gardening. The species epithet was adapted from a Brazilian common name of the tree. The plant has a great number of common names—*jicaro*, *güiro*, *totumo*, *poporo*, and *cuieira* among them, with the first one apparently having the widest usage. This word has been traced to an Aztec or Nahuatl word, *xicalli*, which was applied to a vessel made from the gourd. The vessel became *jicara* in Spanish, and the tree, *jicaro*. The word *güiro*, or *higüero*, widely used in the Caribbean, is the Hispanicized form of an Arawak Indian word.

Probably the first Europeans to see the tree were Columbus and his men. Gourds were seen to be used as water containers and for bailing boats in the Bahamas, but we can't be certain that these were not bottle gourds. The first good description of the plant and its uses was given us by Gonzalo Fernández de Oviedo y Valdés, who came to the Americas in 1514. In his *Historia General y Natural de las Indias*, he tells us, among other things, that the *higüero* is a great tree, more or less like the mulberry of Castille. The fruits are round or somewhat elongate, the round ones being used to make cups for drinking and other purposes. The largest of the fruits will hold a gallon *(dos açumbres)* or more of water. Precious vessels of the gourds are found in Costa Rica and Panama with handles of gold; so beautiful are they that a mighty king might drink from them without reproach. The wood of the tree is flexible and strong and is used for making chairs and for other purposes. In cases of necessity, he further tells us, the Indians eat the fruit.

Following Oviedo, the trees, and particularly the cups, or jicaras, made from them, were to attract the attention of a number of Spanish visitors to the Americas. The cups received special mention, no doubt, because chocolate, a beverage new to the Spanish, was drunk from them. In fact, the word *jicara* was introduced into Spain and became used for any type of cup from which chocolate was drunk. Jicaras are still widely used as cups in tropical America, and in places it is a common sight to see the natives carrying the cups, often attached to their belts, with them.

Vessels made from the gourds could be used, of course, in the same way as almost any vessel. The early Spanish writers mention a number of other uses. Among some of the most noteworthy were as tribute payments to various rulers, for panning gold, for collecting the blood from sacrificial victims, and in warfare. For the last the Indians used the gourds as receptacles for burning chili peppers whose fumes were supposed to drive off the Spanish invaders; or the gourds would be strewn along a path so that when the Spanish approached in the night they would run into them and the noise would announce the presence of the Spanish to the Indians. The last I find a little hard to accept, unless the gourds were filled with stones so as to rattle when touched.

Although the sweetish pulp and the seeds of the gourds may have been eaten at times, this does not appear to have been a common practice. The pulp, however, has been widely used in folk medicine. That this plant should have been so used should come as no great surprise, for probably more plants than not have been used in folk medicine. The principal use of the tree gourd in this regard appears to be for colds and related ailments, for which purpose the pulp is usually made into a syrup, which is drunk. It also reportedly has been used for asthma, diabetes, cuts and internal ab-

Tree gourds (× ca. 1/4). 1, small entire fruit; 2, Cuban jicara; 3, Mexican jicara; 4, Guatemalan jicara; 5, Mexican jicara. (From Kiddle, 1944; courtesy of the Middle American Research Institute of Tulane University.)

Jicaras from Ecuador ($\times$ 1/4).

scesses, as a febrifuge, and as a cure for mange in dogs. The botanist J. N. Rose also recorded another medicinal use in western Mexico. A hole is bored into the gourd, and the pulp and seeds are allowed to dry. Then the gourd is filled with mescal, the alcoholic beverage derived from the maguey plant, which is known locally as *vino tecomate*, or "wine of the gourd." He was told that it was drunk by miners for lung trouble, but "from the quantity which is used and its effects one is inclined to believe that it is taken for other purposes."

The wood of the tree is also valuable, as Oviedo noted.

Maracas and jicaras from Guatemala ($\times$ 1/3).

It is easily worked when fresh and becomes quite hard with age. It is used particularly for ox yokes, tool handles, and stirrups. In nature the tree often supports a large number of epiphytes, or air plants, including orchids. It has been used intentionally as a support for the vanilla orchid in cultivation in Veracruz, and blocks of its wood have proven a good substrate for growing orchids.

Quite probably the tree gourds also had a very early use as rattles, although I have come across no reference to that effect. Rattles made from bottle gourds appear to be one of man's earliest musical instruments. Today gourd rattles, or

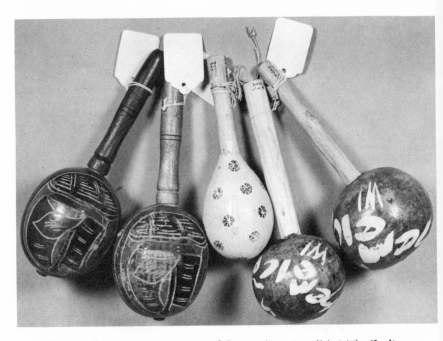

Maracas from various parts of Latin America ($\times$ 1/5). (Indiana University Museum.)

maracas, made from the tree gourd are widely used in Latin music, and many tourists to tropical America bring them home as souvenirs. *Güiros*, or scrapers, another musical instrument, are sometimes made of tree gourds, but more commonly bottle gourds are used.

Visitors will also find decorated jicaras, which can be used as wall hangings or table decorations, sold in markets and tourist shops in many places of tropical America. Polished and engraved jicaras were being made long before the tourists arrived, and we find that usually certain areas of a country specialized in their manufacture. C. V. Hartman has left us a description of the methods used at Izalco, San Salvador. After the gourd is cut and the contents taken out, the epi-

Blowgun dart quiver with tree gourd attached—from Oriente of Ecuador. The gourd holds cotton, which is used to make an airtight seal when placing the dart in the blowgun. (Indiana University Museum.)

dermis is removed and the surface polished with rough leaves until it becomes nearly white. Freehand decorations are then painted on the gourd with a paint brush dipped in beeswax. Following this, a mixture of a gummy solution made from sugar or honey, soot from wood, and boiled pods of a leguminous tree is rubbed over the gourd, giving it a brilliant black color. After it is dry, the gourd is placed in hot water. The heat causes the wax to melt, thereby removing the black color from the parts that had been painted with wax so that the decoration now appears white, or in time yellow. According to Hartman, this method of negative ornamentation was being rapidly supplemented in the late part of the last century by a simpler method in which the design is simply carved in the gourd with a knife. Felix McBryde has left us a good account of this process as observed at Rabenal, Guatemala, in 1943. After the gourd is scoured with leaves, it is covered with a yellow wax, or lacquer, obtained from a scale insect, *Llaveia axin*, which is specially cultivated for its lac wax. Then soot is applied and the gourd polished with a cloth, which gives it a very shiny black finish. The gourd then is engraved by carving on it with a metal instrument to produce lined or geometrical patterns, flowers, birds, or scenes of nature. Sometimes the gourds are engraved without being colored, and sometimes other colors are obtained by using other natural dyes, such as a red from *achiote, Bixa orellana*. Slightly different methods are used in other areas. For example, in Brazil the gourd is painted with a pulverized extract from the bark of two trees that forms a thick brown layer, and upon exposure to the fumes of fermenting urine the brown changes to glossy black. Other accounts state that fermenting or urine-soaked manioc *(Manihot sp.)* leaves are used to secure the black coloration. It may well be that today store-bought paints are used instead of the traditional methods in some places in order to keep up with the tourist demand.

At the outset of this chapter, it was pointed out that there is no difficulty in distinguishing the calabash tree from the bottle-gourd vine; but if one has only the gourds, it is a different matter. The bottle gourd comes in many of the same sizes and shapes as the tree gourd and may be used in the same way. If one makes a very thin section of the gourd rinds and examines them under the microscope, the two may be readily distinguished by the different cellular structures; but for the person who has a gourd at home and wonders which kind it is, a microscopic examination may not be practical. Probably the best test—and it is not absolutely reliable —is to measure a cross section of the rind; that of the tree gourd is three millimeters or less thick, whereas that of the bottle gourd is usually greater. The inside of the tree gourd usually has a smoother finish than that of the bottle gourd; but unless one has the two gourds for comparison, this method of distinguishing them isn't too useful. If the gourd is more than a foot long, it is most likely a bottle gourd, but bottle gourds also come in much smaller sizes. Finally, if a decorated gourd has a very glossy finish, frequently black, it is likely to be a tree gourd rather than a bottle gourd.

Although, as previously pointed out, the bottle gourd and the tree gourd are interchangeable for many uses, some Indian tribes made ceremonial distinction between the two kinds of gourds. The tree gourd was associated with the planet Jupiter and the bottle gourd with the planet Venus. Among the Apenages of Brazil, the bottle gourd could be worn on the head, but the tree gourd couldn't. There also may have been a distinction made in the planting of the two kinds of gourds. In some areas it was the women who planted the seeds of the tree gourds. After doing so in the Oriente of Ecuador, they would strike themselves on their breasts so that the fruits of the trees would grow large like their breasts. No such account is known for the bottle gourd, although women with poorly developed breasts in India are reported to have used bottle gourds as offerings in the temple.

Although the botanist today may not have a complete understanding of the origin of the tree gourd, such is not the case among the Indians of San Salvador, as we learn from a myth.

A man had a wife who was a sorceress and who went out every night to join her lover. However, only her head left the house; her body stayed home. The man asked a friend what he should do. The friend told him to put hot ashes that night where the head should be. The man did so, and when the head returned it couldn't attach itself to its body, but upon catching sight of the husband the head attached itself to his shoulder. The man knew that when a sorceress had landed this way on a body, it was absolutely impossible to get rid of her. After a long time, however, he used a trick to do so. He saw a tree with ripe sapotes, which he knew his wife liked. He asked her to climb down off his shoulder in order that he could climb the tree. She did so, but instead of throwing the ripe fruits to her he threw the hard green ones. The head yelled in pain and jumped on the back of a doe that was passing. The terrified doe ran wildly and finally hurled itself with the head off a cliff. The man returned and told the priest what had happened. The priest told him that he must return and bury the head and take good care of the mound, for surely from this head something good would spring up. Every two weeks the man went to take care of the tomb, and one day he found that a plant was growing from it. Soon it grew into a tree, and one day it bore a flower, which produced a fruit. It was a calabash tree. The man went to the priest and told him what had happened. The priest told him not to touch the fruit until it was ripe. When it finally ripened and fell to the ground, the priest loaned the man a saw to cut it in two. As he was sawing he was quite surprised to hear voices within the shell, and when it was opened he saw four small infants, three boys and one girl. The girl received the name Flower-Girl and grew up to be the most beautiful woman who ever existed. "No man will ever touch me," she said, "but after my death, all the people will enjoy the glorious force which is in me." True to her word, she died a virgin, and from her grave sprang a plant which is more divine than any other plant in the world— tobacco.*

Another story of the origin of the tree gourd is found in the Popol Vuh, the sacred book of the ancient Quiché Mayas

---

*This myth, which is taken from Hartman (see References, Chapter 3), has been considerably condensed in retelling here. I would make two observations: (1) The finding of people in gourds is also encountered in myths in which the bottle gourd figures. (See the last chapter.) (2) The association of tobacco, a sacred plant to many Indians, with the gourd is of interest, for the gourd sometimes served as a receptacle for the tobacco and itself was regarded as sacred. The sacred tobacco gourd of the Huichols of Mexico, however, was a small bottle gourd and not a tree gourd.

of Guatemala. Hun-Hunahpu and his brother, who figure in the Third Creation, were put to death by the Lords of Xibalba, the Maya underworld. They were buried, but first the Lords severed Hun-Hunahpu's head and placed it in a tree. The tree, which had been fruitless, now produced gourds. Hun-Hunahpu's head came to look exactly like the other fruits, and the tree came to be called the gourd tree. The Lords of Xibalba decreed that no one must pick its fruit. A maiden by the name of Xquic, or Blood Girl, heard of the tree and went by herself to see it. "What if I were to take one of the fruits?" she thought. Then the skull spoke to her and told her to reach out. She did so and the gourd spat upon her hand. "From my spittle," the skull said, "I have left you my descendants;" and the girl conceived. Later when her father realized she was pregnant, he asked her to explain. He did not believe her story. So it was ordered that she be taken away and sacrificed, and her heart returned in a gourd bowl. But she tricked him by substituting the red sap of a plant for the blood of her heart. And thus the Lords of Xibalba were defeated by a girl.

A second species of the calabash tree, *Crescentia alata*, which is found from Mexico to Costa Rica, has much smaller fruits. One type is reported to have gourds no larger than a hen's egg; these are used as tops by children in Guatemala. Its fruits are also employed in many of the same ways as those of *Crescentia cujete* and are particularly used for cups. Although often known by the same common names, *Crescentia alata* does have a distinctive name, *morro*, in parts of Middle America. The species is readily identified by its leaves. In *Crescentia cujete* the leaf is undivided, whereas in *Crescentia alata* it is three-parted, more or less in the form of a cross, and has a winged stalk (hence *alata*, which means "winged," for the specific epithet). Oviedo was impressed by the leaf; he wrote that this leaf in the shape of a cross seems very noteworthy and appears to be a testimony of the Cross, of which these people could not have been ignorant. Marveling upon the leaves, he collected some to show in Europe and still had some in his possession at the time of writing his book. The good Catholic Spaniards might marvel at these leaves, but before the coming of the Spanish it is hardly likely that the Indians did, or at least not for the same reason.

Before concluding the discussion of the tree gourd, some comments on the gourde, the monetary unit of Haiti, are called for. For some years I had wondered about the connection of gourde with gourds, and from which gourd it might be derived. Most of the information that I was able to find comes from Chapter 9 of John W. Vandercook's *Black Majesty* (Harper & Row, 1928), from which I have extracted the following.

Henri Christophe became governor of northern Haiti in 1807. At the time the country was bankrupt, but according to Vandercook:

Food grew wild or with little urging. For utensils, bowls, spoons and bottles, the blacks made use of the gourd vine. . . . If there was such a thing as an irreplaceable necessity in the . . . life of the peasants, it was the gourd, Christophe mused. Gourds were useful but they soon wore out. . . . [So] Chief Christophe issued an arbitrary act which declared every green gourd in northern Haiti the property of the state. A new crop was just ripening and soldiers were sent to every commune to collect it. The peasants made no objections. Christophe was their master now and whatever he did was right.

Gourd vines grew over many garden walls. . . . Another sort grew on prim, round-headed little trees. Without regard for quality or ownership, Christophe's messengers took them all and a great procession of laden burros and high-piled farm carts brought them into Cap Haitien. Before long 227,000 green gourds and calabashes were deposited in "The Treasury," Christophe put a value of twenty sous on each. . . [and] to this day the standard coin of Haiti is called the *gourde*.

On first reading this I thought that perhaps it might have the same standing as the story of George Washington's cutting down the cherry tree, but in the introduction Vandercook states that he had omitted nothing except a few foolish legends that had no historical basis. So the story may well be based on fact, and the citation of the exact number of gourds might bear this out, but as the author gives no references I have not been able to verify it. From this account it appears that both the bottle gourd from the "vines [that] grew over many garden walls" as well as the tree gourd from "prim, round headed little trees" were involved.

A more recent and rather brief account is found in Ruth D. Wilson's *Here is Haiti* (1957). Of the calabash tree, she writes that the peasants eat the meat of calabashes, also called gourds, "although they are much larger than the gourds that grow on vines" (what she means by the vine gourd is not clear). A small kind is used to make rattles, called *açons*, for the voodoo priests; another kind is used to make the *tchatchas*, or rattles, used in the native orchestras. "In fact, the calabashes were so useful and common that Christophe . . . decreed they should be used as a medium of exchange after the Revolution when coins were rare."

Her account would indicate the gourde is derived from the tree gourd. In an effort to learn the truth of this matter, I sent letters to the Consulate General of Haiti in New York and the Organization of American States. I have never had replies, which I hope indicates that these people have more important matters to occupy their attention.

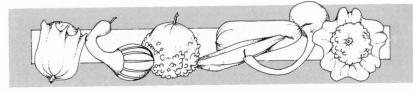

4.
The Cucurbita Gourds

The genus *Cucurbita* includes the pumpkins and squashes and several different kinds of gourds. One of these, the ornamental gourd, is probably the most widely grown gourd in the United States. The great variety of fruits found in this gourd makes it a delight to the eye, but other than that it is one of the most useless of the gourds and at times may even "contaminate" squashes and pumpkins.

The name *Cucurbita* comes from a Latin word for *gourd*, which also carried the meanings of "fool," "idiot," and "adulteress." Apparently the last meaning came from the fact that if adultery were committed and the woman became pregnant her abdomen would swell like a pumpkin. But it couldn't have been in reference to the plant that we know as pumpkin, for no members of the genus *Cucurbita* were known to the Romans. There were no pumpkins for Halloween before the discovery of America; a hollowed-out turnip seems to have served as the original jack-o'-lantern in Ireland.

In addition to the cultivated species of *Cucurbita*, four of which are grown in the United States for food, there are several wild species with gourdlike fruits. Five of these wild species are found in the United States, one of which, the

Buffalo gourd.

buffalo gourd, has a wide distribution and will receive more detailed treatment. Two species occur in the extreme Southwest; one, *C. texana*, is found in Texas and is to be discussed with the ornamental gourds; and another one, *C. okeechobeenis*, named for the lake, is from southern Florida. Dr. L. H. Bailey had made many trips to Florida to collect this gourd, but he was never successful in finding the female flowers. In 1929, accompanied by E. G. Hume, he went again, and this time he was rewarded with the sight of a female flower; however, it was growing thirty feet or more above the ground and hanging over water. But to let him tell the story:

We could find nothing long enough to reach it. The vine would not rip loose. The tree was covered with poison ivy. The day was dark and the tail end of a hurricane was blowing itself out. Hume had a 22 Colt automatic pistol, woodsman model. He climbed the tree a short distance to get above the brush and gripped himself

Key to Cucurbita Gourds

Leaves triangular, usually not lobed,
whitish or grayish-green; wild plants

1. Buffalo gourd
(C. foetidissima)

Leaves roundish or, if triangular,
usually lobed; leaves green; cultivated
plants.
    Stems rather soft, round; fruit stalk
      somewhat spongy or soft corky

2. Turban gourd
(C. maxima)

    Stems rather hard, usually some-
      what angular
      Fruit stalk enlarged and some-
      what hard corky; leaves and
      stems with soft hairs; leaves
      often white-blotched; seeds
      with bluish or grayish border

3. Silver-seed gourd
(C. mixta)

    Fruit stalk not particularly en-
      larged or corky; leaves and
      stems with rather stiff hairs;
      leaves usually not white-
      blotched; seeds without con-
      spicuously colored border.
      Leaves nearly circular in
        outline, with shallow
        rounded lobes; seeds
        black or buff colored;
        perennial

4. Fig-leaf gourd
(C. ficifolia)

      Leaves somewhat triangular,
      usually sharply triangu-
      larly lobed; seeds white to
      buff colored; annual

5. Ornamental gourd
(C. pepo)

tight. Then he fired away. A bullet cut the stem cleanly and the flower floated to my feet in perfect condition. . . . (See References, Chapter 4.)

This is not the only time that gunfire has been the last resort to collect a plant, for I have heard of botanists shooting down orchids in the tropics.

To introduce our cast of characters I submit the key on page 32.

The Buffalo Gourd

When I made my first trip to the southwestern United States in 1942, I noticed in many places a most striking plant, several feet long, with distinctive triangular grayish-green leaves. The bus never stopped in a place where I could examine it, so it was not until sometime later that I learned it was the *buffalo gourd*, also called *calabazilla* and *Missouri gourd*. The scientific name of the plant is *Cucurbita foetidissima*, or "very fetid," a most apt name, for nearly all parts of the plant are ill-smelling. One has only to brush against a leaf to pick up the odor.

The buffalo gourd is a perennial, with a huge root producing trailing vines often twenty feet long. The fruits, which are green-striped when young and yellow at maturity, may reach ten inches in diameter, although more frequently they are only half that size. Although it is not recommended as an ornamental, chiefly because of its ill smell, its unusual appearance would make it of interest in the gourd garden as a novelty. This species grows naturally in rather dry, barren places from Missouri and Nebraska to Texas and California, extending into Mexico.

The seeds were sometimes eaten by Indians of the Southwest, usually in the form of mush. But its other uses appear to have been more important. The plant contains a saponin that produces suds, so it may be used as a soap. Pieces of the root and the fruit were used both as a hand and laundry soap by Indians in southern California, but one report states that the soap is so strong that it can cause skin irritation if particles cling to clothing. It was also used as a shampoo and as a bleach. The plant was widely used in medicine, particularly for open sores on humans and horses. The Omaha Indians believed the plant had mystic properties. Only special people were authorized to dig it; other people were even afraid to handle it. The root was considered to have the form of the human body; hence, that part of the root that corresponded to the part of the body that was ill could be used to cure it. This belief recalls the stories surrounding the mandrake in the Near East and Europe. The gourds were sometimes used for rattles, but their thin shell made them inferior to the bottle gourd for this purpose. The fruits were also used to make ladles and syringes for female douches.

The seeds contain an appreciable amount of oil and have a fairly high protein content, and the huge root produces an abundance of starch. For these reasons, attempts are now under way to develop the plant into a food crop for arid or semiarid regions.

The Turban Gourd

The annual species, *Cucurbita maxima* ("largest"), includes a large number of autumn and winter squashes, the varieties buttercup, banana, and Hubbard being among the most familiar. Some varieties may reach huge sizes, over three hundred pounds, and are the largest fruits of all plants. One group of this species, sometimes distinguished as variety *turbaniformis*, includes the turkscap, or turk's turban, gourd. The name is very apt. In addition to the unusual shape caused by the central part of the ovary being surrounded by the persistent corolla to produce three protuberances, its colors, with reds and oranges predominating, make it an interesting, if not attractive, object to behold. I have seen these gourds over one foot in diameter, although they are usually somewhat smaller. The color will last several months, and then

Silver-seed gourd vine with flower and fruit.

they usually decay, although I have had some dry up completely. Other than being ornamental, they also may be eaten, but many other squashes are to be preferred for that purpose as far as I am concerned.

The Silver-Seed Gourd

In his *Manual of Cultivated Plants*, Bailey places the silver-seed gourd in *Cucurbita argyrosperma* ("silver-seeded"), but T. W. Whitaker, another authority on cucurbits, considers it nothing more than a form of *Cucurbita mixta* ("mixed"), the species that also includes the cushaw squashes. The silver-seed gourd is an extremely vigorous grower and nearly covers a garden before the season is over. The ones that I have grown had oval or pear-shaped green-and-white-striped fruits nearly a foot in diameter. But it is the seeds that are most noteworthy. They are over an inch long and have a distinct

Fig-leaf gourd vine.

darkish band, or rim, around them. I suppose with some stretch of the imagination this band could be called silvery, but in the ones that I have seen the bands are more of a grayish or bluish color. This gourd is apparently more frequently grown in Europe than in the United States, but the original source is probably Mexico.

The Fig-Leaf Gourd

The fig-leaf, or Malabar, gourd also is little grown in the United States. The scientific name is *Cucurbita ficifolia*, which means "fig-leafed," and indeed the plant has leaves similar to those of the common fig tree. For a long time this species was thought to be native to Asia, but its American origin is now established beyond a doubt. In contrast to the other cultivated species, it is a perennial rather than an annual, but when grown where there are hard frosts it does not live over winter. It is also a species that is adapted to high altitudes. I am best acquainted with it from highland Ecuador, where its vines are a common sight. In fact, it often escapes from cultivation and may be seen on vacant lots around Quito, where a single plant will cover a lot in a short time. The fruits, which will last for well over a year, are a common sight in the markets as well as in the countryside where they are often placed on top of roofs to ripen in the sun. The fruit is oblong to nearly globular at maturity and dark green or green with white stripes or blotches. Some friends of mine, newly arrived in Ecuador, bought a fruit in the market thinking it was watermelon and didn't discover their mistake until they cut it open and found the flesh to be white. Although I was aware that the fruits were used for preparing desserts, which I have tried, and that the toasted seeds, like those of some of the other species, are eaten, I had no detailed information on its uses. So I wrote to my friend Jorge Soria, who was born in Ecuador, has traveled widely in Latin America, and now is a resident of Costa Rica, and he replied as follows.

Regarding the ways that *zambo*, *chiverre*, or *lacayote* [names by which the fig-leaf gourd is known in Latin America] is eaten, your information is correct. In Central America it is used mainly to prepare a *dulce*, or preserve. In Costa Rica it is eaten as a *dulce*, which is called *conserva*, only during *Semana Santa* [Holy Week]. In the Andean countries, it has several other uses: (1) The seeds are peeled, roasted, and mashed to make a kind of gravy that is used on potatoes and meat; the roasted seeds are also eaten as *maiz tostado*. (2) The most extensive use by the Indian and campesino population, all year long, is of the immature *zambo* to prepare soups, called *locro de zambo*. They pick the fruits before they attain full size; if the fingernail will penetrate the rind, and if an abundant, clear gummy sap flows from the wound, then it is good for use. The most common soup is made by removing the rind, eliminating the seeds, then making small pieces of the immature fibers and cooking them with potatoes, salt, and spices.

Ornamental gourd with male (left) and female flowers.

(3) The other common use of the mature *zambo* (when the finger-nail cannot penetrate the rind) is to remove the rind and the seeds, make small pieces of the fibrous flesh, and cook it with *panela* (brown sugar), milk, and cinnamon; this is used as a custard dessert.

The Ornamental Gourds

What I call the *ornamental gourd* and Bailey calls the *yellow-flowered gourd* belongs to *Cucurbita pepo—pepo* being an old Latin word for the fruit of an edible melon, now generally used for the fruit of almost any cucurbit. This species comprises the summer squashes, including pattypan and yellow crookneck; the vegetable marrows, such as zuccini; the winter

Finger, or crown-of-thorns, gourds.

squashes, such as acorn; and our orange pumpkins. It is widely grown for these edible fruits as well as gourds. The gourds are placed in a distinct variety, *C. pepo* var. *ovifera* ("egg bearing"), this name having originally been given to them as a species by Linnaeus.

Unlike many of the other gourds included in this book, the ornamental gourds are not edible. The little flesh they may have is rather tasteless, sometimes even bitter. They are not entirely without practical value, however, for I have heard of some people using them as darning eggs for mending socks as well as for nest eggs. They are nearly always grown, however, because they are curious and attractive. A bowl of these gourds makes a fine decoration for a table. Moreover, they

39

Warted ornamental gourds.

are favorites in the United States for the ease with which they can be grown, and they produce rather small vines that will not take over a garden as many of the other gourds do.

The fruits are usually rather small, sometimes no larger than a hen's egg, more commonly three to five inches long or round, rarely nearly a foot long. They also come in a variety of shapes and colors. Bailey gives the shapes as egg, apple, orange, pear, bell, spoon, ladle, and finger. The *finger gourd*, also called *crown-of-thorns gourd, gourd of the Ten Commandments,* and *holy gourd,* is perhaps the most unusual, for on its upper surface it bears five pairs of protuberances, or prongs. The finger gourds that I have grown have been white or cream-colored at maturity. In addition to these

Star gourds.

colors, other kinds are known to be orange, green-and-white-striped, and bicolored, that is, green or green-striped with areas or bands of yellow. The surface of the gourd is usually smooth, but warted forms are not uncommon. The latter at times are very similar to some of the bottle gourds, but have thinner rinds.

These gourds will mix or intercross quite readily, so if one grows several different kinds together and saves the seed, the next season he may well find some new types or intermediates that are hybrids from the previous year. At the Ohio Gourd Show in 1975 I saw a number of types that were not classified by Bailey and were new to me. The exhibitors called these *star gourds*. They came in various colors and

A basket of bicolored spoon gourds for sale in a local market.

sizes; some were warted and others smooth. They were consistent in having ten prominent ridges, or protuberances, on the sides, although there was considerable variation in the nature of these ridges. Their origin is unknown to me, but I suspect that they are hybrids involving the pattypan squash or finger gourd as one parent and various other kinds of gourds as the second parent.

The bicolored gourds are among the most interesting of all the gourds. The first one I ever saw had a perfectly straight band of yellow about a half inch in width around the neck, and I thought it had been secured by using masking tape so that this part wouldn't be exposed to the light. Only later did I learn that it was Nature's work. The bicolored gourds are most unpredictable, for one never knows how much yellow there will be and where it will appear, and there is often great variation in the fruits of a single plant. The inheritance of the fruit color has been studied, and it is most complicated. The bicolor pattern is an example of variegation. A nuclear instability causes a breakdown of the green pigment in some cells on the fruit's surface so that a yellow color results. This character is unstable genetically, and the mutation that causes it is apparently reversible. However, by inbreeding and selection it has been found possible to secure a line of gourds with almost completely yellow fruits.

It is still believed by some farmers that gourds can "contaminate" melons and other cucurbitaceous plants growing near them so that they are unfit to eat. We find this mentioned by Cotton Mather in 1716 when he wrote about a friend of his near Boston whose garden was robbed of squashes on occasion.

To inflict a pretty little punishment on the Theeves, he planted some *Guords* among the Squashes, (which are in aspect very like 'em) at certain places which he distinguished with a private mark, that he might not be himself imposed upon. By this method, the Thieves were deceived, & discovered, & ridiculed. But yet the honest man saved himself no squashes by ye Trick; for they were so infected and Embittered by the Guords, that there was no eating of them.

Also, in a letter from a "J. B." (possibly John Bartram) in *Gentlemen's Magazine* in 1755 one reads: "If we plant cucumbers, squashes, or melon, near the bitter gourd, the fruits of the first will be as bitter as gall . . . this shows how liable plants are to be bastardized by bad neighbors." Both of these accounts—which I have taken from Conway Zirkle's *The Beginnings of Plant Hybridization* (University of Pennsylvania Press, 1935)—imply that the pollen of the gourd (and we can't be sure from the accounts exactly which gourd is meant) influences the taste of the fruits of other cucurbitaceous plants grown near them. For this reason, to this day some farmers will not plant gourds near their squash.

So far as I can learn there has been no scientific verification that the pollen of gourds could have any such effect, and it would hardly be expected to have any. I have never conducted any experiments myself, but I have grown many kinds of gourds near squash without any ill effects on the fruits of the latter. If, however, one were to grow ornamental gourds near summer squash (or other varieties of *Cucurbita pepo*) and plant the seeds from the squash the next year, it is quite possible that the plants secured would be hybrids between the gourd and squash and would scarcely be edible. Perhaps Mather and J. B. were actually referring to such, but had the effect occur one year too early.

The ornamental gourds of which we have been speaking are truly domesticated plants in that they are perpetuated only by man, but there is a very similar gourd that grows wild in parts of Texas that many botanists recognize as a distinct species, *Cucurbita texana*. It differs very little from the ornamental gourds except that it grows without man's aid. Hybrids that have been made between it and the ornamental gourds are fully fertile. Thus it appears that there may be little reason for regarding it as a distinct species. Some have held that *Cucurbita texana* is nothing more than an escaped ornamental gourd that has reverted to a wild existence. Others believe that it is a truly wild plant and probably very similar to the ancestor of *Cucurbita pepo*. There is, at present, no evidence for deciding which of these theories is correct. Other botanical evidence suggests that the cultivated pumpkins and squashes belonging to *Cucurbita pepo* were first domesticated in Mexico. It could, of course, be that the Texas gourd at one time had a distribution that extended into Mexico, where it has since become extinct and survives today only in Texas.

It seems likely that all of the cultivated squashes and pumpkins were derived from gourdlike ancestors. The question can be raised as to why early man ever sought to cultivate these gourds, for what little flesh they have is extremely bitter. It has been suggested that they were first cultivated for the edible seeds. Then under cultivation mutants occurred that resulted in a greater development of flesh, and other mutants, in nonbitterness, so that in time the plants were cultivated primarily for their flesh and only secondarily for their seeds.

Flowering plants have evolved a number of very efficient ways for dispersing their seeds by wind, water, or animals. Winged seeds or fruits are scattered by the wind. The seeds of the maple and the ash are well-known examples. Seeds or fruits that float, such as the coconut and bottle gourd, are susceptible to dispersal by water. Seeds or fruits such as beggar's lice or Spanish needles, which stick to the coats or feathers of mammals and birds, are dispersed by animals. Other fruits are attractive to animals as food, and the seeds may remain viable after passing through the digestive tract, thus allowing their wide dissemination. The pumpkin is a fruit that is eaten by animals; in fact, it is often used as cattle feed. I do not know if the seeds pass through the animal and, if they do, whether they are viable. It doesn't really matter, for man saves seeds for planting. All of our domesticated plants, including the ornamental gourd, have man as their dispersal agent. The question is, how do wild gourds get around?

Although the dispersal of many plants has been studied, the wild gourds appear to have escaped any detailed investigations. Some speculation may be in order, however. Their spherical shape might allow them to roll some distance, but this would hardly be significant in most places. They also can float when they are dry, but this can hardly be important to the many species that grow in rather arid regions unless they inhabit banks of streams or are in the path of flash floods. Even though the bitterness of gourds makes them unpalatable to man, it is possible that some animals may eat them and scatter some of the seeds. The seeds are probably eaten by rodents, but certainly some would escape such a fate. A single gourd plant will produce several branches that may extend for many feet in several directions; thus, the fruits will be borne at some distance from where the parent plant was originally established. Eventually these rather brittle fruits may be broken, exposing the seeds. It could well be that the wild gourds have no specialized means of dispersal. Nevertheless, they seem to get around very well, for some wild gourds, such as the buffalo gourd, have a very wide distribution.

Although I have worked with domesticated plants for over thirty years, I still never cease to marvel at the great diversity that may be found in one species. *Cucurbita pepo* is a good example, for within this single species we find a number of different kinds of pumpkins, squashes, and, particularly, gourds. The other parts of the plants that bear these fruits, however, show far less diversity than do the fruits. Domesticated plants as a whole display their greatest diversity in that character for which man grows them, as was pointed out by both Alphonse de Candolle and Charles Darwin more than a century ago. Thus, in corn it is the grain; in beans, the seeds; in petunias, the flowers; and in cucurbits, the fruits that show the greatest diversity. Wild plants seldom, if ever, show the same great range of types within a single species. How then do we account for the greater variation in domesticated species? Gene mutations occur in both wild and cultivated plants. If, let us say, a mutant occurred that affected the fruit shape or color of a cucurbit, man (or more likely woman) was drawn to it and saved the seed for planting the next season, and thus the mutant could be perpetuated. Such a mutant may also have arisen in the wild, but it may have had little chance of surviving, unless it conferred some benefit to the species. Furthermore, it is possible that man carried his mutant type to a new area where another mutant type was known. If both types were grown together, spontaneous hybridization could have occurred, and eventually recombinant types might have appeared that were different from either of the original parents. Thus, gene mutation, recombination

46

following crossing, and selection by man (or artificial selection as opposed to natural selection) can account for the great diversity found in so many of man's domesticated plants, including *Cucurbita pepo* and the bottle gourd, as well, as we shall see in a later chapter.

Ridged loofah in flower.

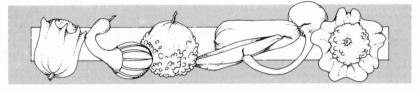

5.
The Loofahs

As I was glancing through the Sunday supplement section of the local newspaper in the spring of 1975, a full-page advertisement caught my attention. In big print the headline read, *"At last! The Amazing Oriental Plant That Helps Wipe Away Ugly Cellulite In Just Minutes A Day!"* To be honest, I must say that I'm not sure it was the headline that caught my attention; it may have been the drawing of a beautiful girl, in a barely adequate bathing suit, stretched out across the page. In any event I read on. "Fights sagging jaw line and 'turkey neck,' destroys upper arm flab. Banishes crocodile skin. Wipes away orange peel buttocks. Nothing can banish ugly cellulite bumps except this treatment. Diets alone can't do it. Exercise alone can't do it. Even surgery can't do it." I didn't know what cellulite was, but there was a box with a photograph of a woman squeezing some cellulite on her leg, and the explanation that cellulite was "fatty deposits that have gone astray" and cling to "the most obvious parts of a woman's body." As I read on I learned that the loofah pad with its thousands of tiny fingers can eliminate cellulite. And on and on it went about the marvelous properties of the loofah. "Could this be the loofah gourd?" I asked myself. The drawing of the plant that was shown hardly resembled it; but "the story of the loofah" left little doubt, for it said that the plant belonged to the cucumber family and originated in India. About a half century ago, it went on, a Korean king issued an order that a sponge be found, good for cleaning the body but that would not scratch the skin. His men soon brought him the loofah, and from that time on it became the royal bath sponge. In the corner of the page was the usual order form, and I found that a loofah pad could be secured for $3.98 plus 50 cents postage. The price seemed a bit high to me, for a few days earlier I had seen one advertised in one of my wife's novelty catalogues for $2.50—but it didn't promise to remove cellulite. Later I saw some selling for even less in a local store.

Although the claims about removing cellulite may be exaggerated, it is generally agreed by its devoted users that the loofah sponge is most invigorating. Other advantages that it possesses over the more traditional washcloth is that if after use it is placed in a position for ventilation, it dries quickly, never develops a sour odor, and never needs to be laundered. My wife, who has offered them for sale at church bazaars, finds that, although people are often reluctant to experiment with them initially, a very high percentage of those who do purchase one repeatedly request them in subsequent years. But there is no need to buy them if one has a garden, for they are not particularly difficult to grow.

There are two species of the loofah that are fairly widely cultivated, *Luffa aegyptiaca*, the common loofah, and *Luffa acutangula*, the ridged loofah. Both the common name and the genus name come from an Arabian word for the plant. Other common names often encountered are *sponge gourd*, *rag gourd*, and *dishcloth gourd*. *Luffa aegyptiaca*, or the "Egyptian loofah," is called *Luffa cylindrica* in the older literature. In spite of its specific epithet, this loofah, as well as *Luffa acutangula*, originally comes from Asia, and both species are perhaps native to India. The two species are easily distinguished.

Luffa aegyptiaca, the more common of the two in this country, has deeply lobed leaves and rather large, bright yellow flowers that open in the morning. The male flowers may reach five inches in diameter. The fruits are somewhat cylindrical in shape, usually a foot to a foot and a half in length, and have been reported to reach lengths of six feet, which I find a little hard to believe. The flat, oval seeds, about one-half-inch long, are black, or rarely nearly white, and smooth, with a slight rim on the margin.

Luffa acutangula has more shallowly lobed leaves and smaller pale yellow flowers that open in the evening. The fruits are somewhat club-shaped, definitely ridged or angled (hence the name *acutangula)* on the surface, and generally somewhat smaller than those of the previous species. The seeds are black, slightly more elongate than in *Luffa aegyptiaca*, with a pitted surface and lacking a rim.

The fruit, or gourd, of both species is green until it changes to a yellow-tan or nearly brown color as it matures. The rind, or outer layer, of the fruit is almost papery and may be peeled off at maturity, quite readily so if the fruit is soaked in water for a few days. Removal of the rind reveals the fibrous network for which there are so many uses. This fibrous skeleton is much stronger and rougher in *Luffa aegyptiaca* than in *Luffa acutangula*, which has given the former species the greater economic importance.

In addition to cleaning the body, the fibrous interior of the fruit has been used for cleaning glassware, dishes, and kitchen utensils in much the same way a scouring pad or an ordinary coarse sponge may be used. It is ideal for scouring no-stick pans because it easily scrapes off stuck food without scratching the surface of the pan. It has also been used to make pot holders, table and door mats, sandals and insoles. Flattened by being pressed through steam rollers, it has been used to make soundproof wall boarding. It has good insulation properties and has been used to make sun helmets and as a lining for steel army helmets. It makes a good packing material and has also been used for stuffing mattresses and saddles. It has

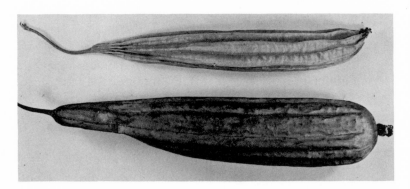

Fruits of loofahs: above, ridged loofah; below, common loofah.

Fruits of loofahs with rind removed to show fibrous interior: above, ridged loofah; below, common loofah.

also been found extremely fine for making filters for steam engines and diesel motors.

The plant was first grown commercially in Japan in the early 1890's. Before World War II the United States imported large amounts, 60 per cent of which was utilized for filters. With the coming of the war, when imports from Japan were cut off, it became a strategic material, and commercial production was begun in tropical America. After the war, however, Japan again became the principal supplier and has more or less maintained a monopoly because it has produced the best gourds for commercial use. However, the loofah has never regained its prominence for use in filters in the United States.

The immature fruit of *Luffa* is used for food in southeastern Asia and the Orient and is sometimes sold in Chinese food markets in the United States. *Luffa acutangula* is much favored over *Luffa aegyptiaca* for this purpose. The fruits are usually eaten when only four inches long. They are very popular in India, where they are often an ingredient in curries. In India a wild form of this species occurs, whose fruits are much smaller and extremely bitter. The larger size and the loss of bitterness in the cultivated forms thus appear to be characteristics that developed under selection by man. There are also a few reports of the fruits of *Luffa aegyptiaca* being eaten, but apparently bitterness is more widespread in this species than in the former, which makes it less acceptable for food. As the bitter types may also be somewhat toxic, caution should be exercised if one tries to use his home-grown loofahs for food.

Various parts of the plant of both species have been employed in folk medicine. The seeds are emetic and purgative. The fiber of the fruit and pulverized ripe fruit have been used in China for a number of ailments. Leaves have been used in the treatment of skin diseases. The juice extracted from the stems has been used for respiratory complaints and, even more so, as a toilet water. The juice is highly regarded in Japan for anointing the body to soften the skin and is sold commercially for this purpose.

An artificial hybrid between the species was reported some years ago; as I have made the hybrid myself, I can give some firsthand information. When pollen of *Luffa aegyptiaca* is applied to the stigmas of *Luffa acutangula*, good seed set results. These seeds give rise to vigorous hybrids, which, as is to be expected, are more or less intermediate between the parents in appearance. The hybrids produced numerous fruits; but when the fruits were opened, they were found to contain only one or two filled seeds in each, whereas the parents normally produce around 100 seeds. I found that the seeds from the hybrids would germinate, but the plants they produced were not vigorous and failed to produce fruits.

Thus far the discussion has centered around the cultivated species. The genus contains about six other species—I say "about," for there has been no recent scientific study of the genus and it is impossible to be sure how many of these species deserve recognition. These species have a rather interesting distribution. Four of them are native to the Old World tropics and two to the Americas. The latter are quite distinct from the Old World species. The genus probably had its origin in the Old World; how the progenitor of the American species arrived here poses an interesting problem.

The two cultivated species are now widely grown in tropical America, where they were introduced by man in post-Columbian times. Thus, they could hardly have given rise to the native American species, one of which seems to have been used by the Aztecs before America was "discovered." The fruits of the loofahs apparently will float for only a short time, so it seems unlikely that the fruits were carried to the Americas by ocean currents. The seeds, however, of one species have been reported to float for months. It seems highly unlikely to me that seeds could have floated across the Pacific Ocean, found a satisfactory place to grow, and still retained viability. But perhaps this is the explanation— only one seed would have to be successful, for the plant it

Seed dispersal in the common loofah. Lid, or operculum, is still attached to the gourd at left; lid has fallen from gourd at right, allowing the seeds to escape.

Common loofah in home garden.

gave rise to could produce more seeds, which in turn would spread. Tests should be made on the viability of the seeds after long immersion in salt water.

Water, however, does not appear to be the primary method of dispersal for the loofahs. In the two cultivated species, the tip of the fruit breaks off at maturity and the seeds may be shaken out. As the plants often climb for some distance in trees, this method of seed dispersal would allow the seeds to fall out and be carried by wind a short distance from the parent plant. Because the seeds are somewhat trapped by the fibrous network of the fruit, only a few come out at a time, and thus the seeds are released over a long period of time.

Philip Miller in his *Gardener's Dictionary* of 1754 had this to say of the loofah, which he called the Egyptian cucumber: "The fruit, when it is young, is by some people eaten, and made into mango's, and preserved in pickle; but it is not accounted very wholesome: wherefore these plants are seldom cultivated in Europe, except by such persons as are curious in Botany, for variety."

It never did become an important food plant in Europe or the Americas, but it has become important in other ways. I have heard, but have not verified, that not a bathtub is to be found in England without a loofah sponge. With the current advertising campaign, it may soon be the same in the United States, although I have heard some people complain that it is a little too rough for delicate skins. However, if people in these countries don't try the young fruits for food, they may be missing a good thing, for according to a Chinese herbalist of the sixteenth century, "the fresh fruit is considered to be cooling and beneficial to the intestines, warming to the stomach, and tonic to the genital organs."

COLOR PLATES

A prizewinning display at the Ohio Gourd Show in 1975, featuri
ornamental, bottle, and turban gourds.

Turban gourds for sale at a roadside mark

Fig-leaf gour

An assortment of ornamental gourds.

Bicolored gourds. All of these came from a single plar

A common loofah in flowe

A harvest of bottle gourds from the author's garden.

Fruit of the bitter gourd, or balsam pear. The fruit on the left has split open, exposing seeds.

A bottle-gourd flower with visitors—a honey bee and cucumber beetles.

Decorated gourds from Peru.

Inexpensive *matés* and *bombillas* from Argentina.

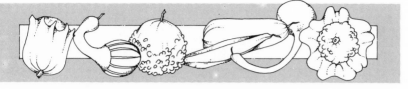

6.
Various Other Gourds

Snake Gourds

The first time I grew the snake gourd* I was very disappointed, for the fruits were not more than five inches long and rather plump, not at all snakelike. The flowers, however, were certainly no disappointment; the delicately fringed white corolla with its delightful aroma is reason enough for growing this so-called snake gourd. Since that time, however, I have grown plants with truly remarkable snakelike fruits.

The genus name of this plant, *Trichosanthes*, from the Greek for "hair flower," is most appropriate. Linnaeus described two species, *Trichosanthes anguina* ("serpent") and *Trichosanthes cucumerina* ("cucumberlike"). Although it is now generally agreed that these two names refer to the same species, the former name is often applied to the wild form of the snake gourd and the latter to the cultivated forms.

The epithet *anguina* is the more descriptive, for the fruits are often long and sometimes curled, green or green with

*Some of the narrow elongate forms of the bottle gourd *(Lagenaria siceraria)* are sometimes referred to as "snake" gourds, but as far as I am concerned they are less entitled to the name. There is also a plant known as the "snake," or "serpent," melon which is a kind of muskmelon *(Cucumis melo).*

Flower of snake gourd ($\times$ 2 1/2).

white stripes when young, then turning a brilliant orange, and finally cardinal red. The ones I have grown have reached nearly five feet in length, but some have been reported almost a foot longer. The epithet *cucumerina* is also not inappropriate, for the gourd was thought to be a kind of cucumber when it first reached Europe. The young fruits are commonly eaten in India and southeastern Asia, boiled, in curries, or as a substitute for French beans. As the fruit ages it becomes bitter and fibrous. Like so many bitter fruits, whether or not they have real value, it has found use in native medicine in southeastern Asia. Several other species are also grown in that part of the world and used medicinally, or as food, or for both purposes.

Libby Smith with fruit of a snake gourd. This fruit, nearly five feet long, was grown in the greenhouse.

Little is known about seed dispersal of the snake gourd. The fruits of the domesticated ones that I have grown simply dry up at maturity and remain hanging on the vines, or the fruit begins to rot and eventually falls to the ground. The bright color of the fruit possibly serves to attract birds or other animals in nature, which may aid in some way in the spread of the seeds. The seeds themselves bear a fleshy red covering. In many plants in which the seeds have such a covering, birds are the primary dispersal agents, but in such plants the seeds are exposed at maturity (the bitter gourd, for example, discussed later in this chapter). The fruit of the snake gourd, however, does not split open at maturity to expose the seeds, so with this gourd, as with so many of the other ones, the exact means of seed dispersal must remain in doubt.

Pollination, like seed dispersal, is of fundamental importance to a species, for without pollination, with a very few exceptions, there will be no seed set. Showy flowers are most often adapted to pollination by insects, as are all of the gourds. No other gourd flower, however, has the delightful fragrance of the snake gourd. The aroma, the fringe, and the white color all probably have a role in attracting pollinators. The flower of the snake gourd opens late at night, at which time the fringe is fully expanded. It starts to close early the next morning except during cool or cloudy weather when it may remain open until nearly noon. I do not know what insects pollinate these flowers in their homeland, but I suspect that night-flying moths may be involved.

I have never had much luck growing snake gourds out-of-doors, but I have had considerable success with greenhouse plants. I have grown them in two different greenhouses, one screened and the other unscreened. In the former, quite naturally, fruits are never produced unless the flowers are pollinated by hand. An abundance of fruits, however, is found on the plants in the unscreened houses, but I have never seen an insect on the female flowers in the morning and I have never stayed up through the night to determine when and how they are pollinated.

Wax Gourds

In giving the common names of plants, I have usually tried to use the one that is most widely used in English; or, if several are widely used, I have tried to select the one that I feel is most appropriate. As already indicated, there are rules that govern the scientific naming of plants, but no laws govern their common names. Thus the same plant may have many different common names, even within the same country. I have adopted the name *wax gourd* for the plant under discussion, although the name *white gourd* is just as appropriate. Another name, *Chinese preserving melon*, is really too long to be readily accepted, but it is given in many books. Other English names that have been used include *white pumpkin, tallow gourd, ash gourd, Chinese watermelon, winter melon,* and *gourd melon.*

Fortunately, we have a scientific name, *Benincasa hispida,* that is the same all over the world. The genus name was given to it by an Italian botanist, Gaetano Savi, in 1818 to honor Giuseppe Benincasa, an Italian patron of botany. He called the plant *Benincasa cerifera,* or "wax bearing," a very good name, for its fruit bears a layer of white wax. This wax has actually been used to make candles. However, the plant had been named *Cucurbita hispida* by Carol Peter Thunberg in 1794. Although wax gourd does appear very much like some of the species of *Cucurbita,* it differs from them in certain technical characters. (See key on page 32.) Therefore, botanists accept it today as a species of the genus *Benincasa,* but use the epithet *hispida* instead of *cerifera,* because the former is the earliest name given to the plant, and names of species follow the rule of priority. *Hispida,* meaning "rough-hairy," is very apt, for nearly all parts of the plant, including the fruit, at least when it is young, are hispid. It should be noted, however, that not all species epithets are appropriate or descriptive, nor is there any rule that they must be.

The wax gourd has little to recommend it as an ornamental. It is, in fact, primarily a food plant, of particular importance in India and China. The oblong to globular fruits may reach lengths of four feet and may be eaten raw like cucumber, but are more commonly consumed as a cooked vegetable or as a sweetmeat, called *heshim* in India, in which pieces of the fruit are coated with sugar or syrup. In China the fruit is often used for soups, the hollowed-out end of the gourd itself sometimes serving as the bowl. The plant has been

Fruits of wax gourd. The white color is due to the wax.

introduced, generally by the Chinese, into many other countries. I found the fruits being sold in the Lima, Peru, wholesale market to supply the local Chinese restaurants. It is fairly widely grown in Cuba today, where the *dulces*, or sweets, made from it are quite popular. The plant was introduced into the United States in 1884, but it has never really caught on here, perhaps because any role it might serve is already well satisfied by our squashes and pumpkins. My family has tried it, and they were not enthusiastic in their praise; but some have felt otherwise, particularly the Florida botanist Julia Morton, who feels that it is an excellent vegetable and deserves more attention.

The fruits are not true gourds, but they do have unusual lasting properties. I harvested one more than two years ago, which not only looks the same as the day I brought it in, but which, judging from its weight, I would say still contains an appreciable amount of water. The plants are vigorous growers and require a large amount of space in the garden as well as a long season of warm weather to produce fruits. In southeastern Asia they are frequently grown on houses, the roofs of which serve as supports for the fruits.

This plant, too, has found a role in folk medicine. The fresh juice of the plant has been used particularly for the treatment of nervous disorders, and the seeds have been used as a vermifuge for tapeworms in India.

Bitter Gourds, or Balsam Pears

Of the plants in this book, the one sometimes called the *bitter gourd* is certainly one of the least gourdlike, but as it bears the name *gourd* and is fairly widely grown, it deserves inclusion here. It is probably better known in English-speaking countries under the name *balsam pear;* although I have seen no explanation of this name, it is probably to be preferred over *bitter gourd,* for, as we have already seen, the name *bitter gourd* is also sometimes used for the colocynth. (See Chapter 2.) This example illustrates another difficulty with common names; not only may they change as we go from region to region, but the same name may be used for completely different plants. Another common name for the balsam pear is *leprosy gourd,* because of its use in the Orient for the treatment of leprosy. However, my favorite name is *maiden's blush,* a West Indian name probably derived from the rosy color of the fruits.

The scientific name is *Momordica charantia.* The genus name comes from a Latin word meaning "to bite," referring to the jagged edge of the seed, which appears as if having been bitten; but the species epithet is not so readily explained. About all I can say is that it is a name used by botanists before Linnaeus for this plant and that he adopted it for this species. The plant has smaller, more delicate foliage than

Fruit of bitter gourd, or balsam pear, starting to dehisce to expose seeds. A color photograph of the bitter gourd follows page 56.

most of the other gourds and hence makes a good ornamental for use as a screen for the porch or on arbors. The rather small flowers, usually lemon yellow, and the fruit, if not particularly attractive, are at least most interesting. The fruit, at first green, changes to an orange or reddish color as it matures; it is usually warted or covered with blunt or rather pointed protuberances. It may reach a foot in length and two and a half inches in width. It never becomes hard, and it splits open at maturity into three valves to expose the seeds, which are covered with a red or scarlet sticky substance, known technically as the aril. The plant is worth growing for no other reason than to see the fruit split open and expose the brightly colored seeds. When I first saw this, I realized that the seeds must be dispersed by birds, the bright red covering being an advertisement to them. Later I learned that the seeds are indeed eaten by birds.

The balsam pear is native to the Old World tropics. Slaves supposedly introduced it to the New World, where it is now fairly common in cultivation and as a weed. The plant has escaped from cultivation in the southern United States and sometimes becomes a nuisance in orange groves by practically covering the trees.

The plant is used for food in many places, particularly in India. The aril of the seed is sweetish and is sometimes eaten, but it is the fruit that is of greatest culinary value. Young fruits are preferred, for the older fruits are bitter and require the removal of seeds and skins as well as treatment to remove the bitter principle by rinsing in boiling water and soaking in salt water. It is used as a green vegetable or stuffed with meat or other vegetables.

It is also extensively used in folk medicine, nearly all parts of the plant being employed in one way or another. As one early writer put it, it "dissipates melancholy and gross humours." Probably the fruit is the part most often employed, being used for chronic colitis, bacillary dysentery, wounds, burns, itches, chilblains, gout, rheumatism, ailments of the liver and spleen, boils, menstrual difficulties, catarrh, coughs, and as a purge or vermifuge. In large doses the fruit is thought to be an abortifacient. The vine has almost as many uses. In Yucatán a tea made from the leaves is regarded as an aphrodisiac. In the West Indies women take it as a birth-control measure, and men take it as an aid to digestion and as an appetizer. Because of the plant's known toxicity, great care must be exercised when it is taken as a medicine. Children have become ill from eating it, and one death has been reported. It has also been suspected in the death of dogs. The plant has also been used in making arrow poison in the Philippines and insecticide in Haiti.

A second species of the genus, *Momordica balsamina*, known as *balsam apple*, is also grown as an ornamental and likewise has been used as a food and in medicine, although to a lesser extent than the balsam pear. It has smaller, less deeply lobed leaves; the bract of the flowering stalk is toothed and borne much nearer the flower; and the fruit is much smaller, only about three inches long.

Still another species, *Momordica cochinchinensis*, known as the *Cochinchin gourd*, has a fruit that Bailey describes as "a densely tuberculate heavy ovoid body six to eight inches long, yellowish at maturity, with strong odor." I am not acquainted with it, and apparently it is not grown in the United States. Bailey tried to grow it at Ithaca, New York, but it did not mature. The fruits and seeds are eaten in southeastern Asia.

The Teasel and the Hedgehog

The *teasel gourd*, *Cucumis dipsaceus* (from *Dipsacus*, the teasel plant), native to northeastern tropical Africa, is grown as an ornamental for its curious fruits, which are ovoid, two to three inches long, yellow at maturity, and densely covered with long, soft spines. I know of no other uses for it. Bailey also gives the name *hedgehog gourd*, but that name today is being used for another species, *Cucumis metuliferus* ("bearing pyramids," apparently in reference to the pyramidlike spines), which is also known under the name *horned cucumber*. Its fruit, which gets to be four to five inches long, does resemble a cucumber and bears a number of rather stout, stiff spines. The fruits become orange or orange-red at maturity, and the numerous seeds are borne in a jellylike pulp. This species is also native to Africa, where the fruit is sometimes eaten.

The genus *Cucumis* also includes such familiar species as the cucumber and melons—cantaloupe, honeydew, casaba, and so on. There are several other wild species of *Cucumis* in Africa with spiny fruits, some of which might also make interesting ornamentals.

One would suppose that the spiny nature of the fruits has some biological significance. The character of a fruit frequently is related in some way to its dispersal. Both the teasel and hedgehog gourds have fleshy fruits, so I assume that the fruits may be eaten by animals. Then why the spines?

Fruits of hedgehog gourd.

Fruits of teasel gourd.

Stiff spines frequently enable fruits to stick to the skin of animals and thereby be dispersed, but the spines in neither of these species would appear to function very effectively in this regard. I have observed that the tip of the spine of the hedgehog gourd becomes less formidable and quite easily broken off as the fruit becomes ripe. Thus it may be that the spines keep the fruit from being eaten until the seeds have reached maturity. At the moment I have no suggestion as to the significance of the spines of the teasel gourd. It would be worthwhile to have some observations of these fruits in nature.

PART II.
THE BOTTLE GOURD

Bottle-gourd plant in fruit. An open male flower is in the center; to its right, a female flower in bud.

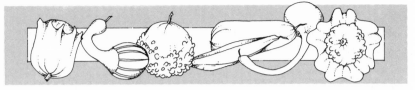

7.
General Considerations

All of the gourds thus far discussed are really of rather minor importance, but now we arrive at *the* gourd.* As Villaneuva has put it, "Estamos . . . en prescencia de una de las maravillas del mundo vegetal: la planta que da bottellas" ("We are in the presence of one of the marvels of the vegetable world: the plant that gives bottles"). Its greatest use has been as a bottle or container for both liquid and dry materials, and for that reason alone it must have been one of man's most important plants before the invention of pottery. But it gives more than bottles and containers. It is also used for food, floats, musical instruments, medicine, artistic endeavors, and as an almost indispensable item in man's attire, as well as in many other ways. I shall address myself to its uses in more detail in later chapters. It was a very widespread cultivated plant in pre-historic times, found throughout the tropics and subtropics of both hemispheres and extending into the temperate zone in some places. Perhaps it was the world's most widely distributed plant in those early times. How it attained such a

---

*And in this and following chapters we shall, for the most part, simply say "gourd" when referring to this species.

wide distribution is a subject that will receive further attention, but first let us examine the name and the plant.

The bottle gourd belongs to the genus *Lagenaria*—from *lagena*, meaning "bottle." In the older literature it is often referred to as *Lagenaria vulgaris* ("common") or *Lagenaria leucantha* ("white-flowered"), but it is now generally agreed that the correct name is *Lagenaria siceraria*, from *sicera*, meaning "drinking vessel." Linnaeus called the plant *Cucurbita lagenaria*.

The plant is a vine, those having smaller fruits sometimes reaching only a few feet in length, but more often than not it is a much larger plant, sometimes attaining lengths of fifty feet or more. The large, soft leaves, entire or shallowly three- to five-lobed, have a very characteristic musky odor when bruised. The showy white flowers, from one to six inches in diameter, open at dusk and close early the following morning, except on cloudy or overcast days. One needs only a single plant to obtain fruits, for pollen from a male flower will function on the female flower of the same plant, as is true of most of the other gourds.

Night-blooming plants with light-colored showy flowers are often pollinated by moths, and I assumed therefore that the gourds in my garden were probably pollinated by the Sphinx moth, which I had often seen pollinating other nearby plants, such as the evening primrose and the Jimson weed. To try to verify this, I spent many an evening and night in the garden, but I never did see a moth on the flowers. I did learn that both in the evening and early morning bees visit the flowers. Honeybees are frequent visitors, but their activities are largely confined to the male flowers; only once did I see one land on a female flower. In fact, I often observed a honeybee approach a female flower, circle it, and then fly on to a male flower. I thought that perhaps they were in search of pollen, but Dr. Paul D. Hurd, Jr., who identified the bees that I had caught on the flowers, found no pollen on their bodies. So it seemed likely that they were seeking only nectar. But why visit only the male flowers? A detailed

Author with dipper gourds. In order for the gourds to have a straight neck, it is necessary to grow them on a trellis or fence.

examination of the flowers provided the answer—the male flowers have nectaries, but the female flowers do not. Bumblebees also visit the flowers, and they too seem to limit their visits largely to male flowers. On a very few occasions in the evening in late summer I have seen hummingbirds visiting the flowers. I could never get near enough to be sure that they never visited female flowers, but I rather think not.

By far the most common visitor to the flowers were small beetles—the striped cucumber beetle (perhaps more correctly known as the "southern corn rootworm") and the spotted cucumber beetle. As soon as the flowers, both male and female, open, these insects are almost always present, and they may still be found in the flowers after they have closed the next day. The insects are apparently using the flowers

73

When dipper gourds are grown on the ground, the necks assume some interesting and unusual shapes.

as a food source, and it is they, I think, who are responsible for most of the pollination of the gourds in my garden.

My observations, of course, tell us nothing about the pollination of gourds in the tropics; perhaps moths do pollinate the gourd there. Information on the pollination conceivably might give us some clues as to the homeland of the gourd. Do the same insects pollinate the gourd in both the New and Old World tropics, and, if so, to which continent are they native?

The fruits of the gourd come in an amazing number of shapes and sizes, probably exceeding that found in any other

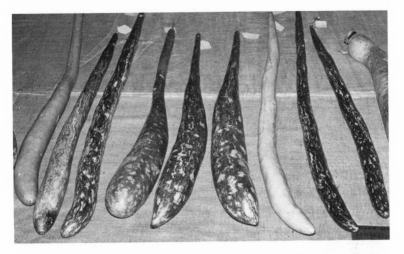

Elongate bottle gourds. The longest measured five feet four inches, not a record by any means. These gourds are sometimes called "snake gourds," but are not to be confused with the snake gourds of an earlier chapter.

member of the family. In size they range from forms smaller than the closed fist to elongate types that are reported to reach nine feet in length and to ovoid types that are more than six feet in circumference. In many areas where they are grown, each fruit type has a distinctive name. In English these are sometimes given as *dumbbell, club, dipper, powder horn, kettle, dolphin,* and *trough gourds,* although this list fails to cover all the various shapes. The color of the mature fruit varies from a very dark to a very light green, almost white; and, although they are usually uniformly colored, both mottled and longitudinally striped forms are known. The gourds are soft-downy when young, but usually become quite smooth when they are mature. Forms are known from both Mexico and South Africa in which the surface is warted,

Susan Kephart and giant gourd, seeds of which came from Ghana.

similar to some of the ornamental gourds; one type, the *maranka*, or dolphin, is definitely ridged.

When young the gourd is fleshy and filled with a white pulp in which the seeds are embedded. As the gourd ages the inner parts dry up, leaving only the seeds. The flesh may be bitter or nonbitter, and only those of the latter type are used for food. I have seen it stated that wild gourds are bitter and domesticated varieties are not, but, quite aside from the fact that no one seems to be sure that there are wild gourds, many of the cultivated types are definitely bitter. The bitter gourds, if they are to be used to hold water or beverages, require special treatment. In parts of Africa water is allowed

Maranka, or dolphin, gourds.

to stand in them for several months until the bitterness has leached out and they may be used as water bottles. In parts of the Pacific the gourds were boiled in order to remove the bitterness. There is a case on record of men having become violently ill after having drunk wine from a gourd. The implication was that it was a bitter gourd and not the wine that was responsible.

In many descriptions of bottle gourds it is stated that the seeds may be distinguished by two hornlike projections on the top, but many kinds lack these. In fact, the seeds are so variable—horned or not, surface smooth or longitudinally lined, margin smooth or corky—that it is difficult to give a

Warted bottle gourds. These are known from both Africa and Mexico.

concise description. The reader is referred to the photographs in the next chapter.

To explain the great diversity of fruit shapes is relatively simple, but it is not easy to account for the great variability in the seeds. As was pointed out in an earlier chapter, a domesticated plant generally shows the greatest variability in that character for which it is cultivated, so it comes as no surprise to find great variability in the fruit of the gourd, for that is the part most widely used by man. Man would deliberately perpetuate new mutant types of the fruit which might well not survive in a strictly wild species. Although the seeds have been used for food, this does not seem to have been an important usage. It might be supposed that the seed variation is strictly a by-product of the fruit variability; actually, except for the fact that large gourds seem to have larger seeds and small gourds smaller seeds, there appears to be no correlation of seed type with fruit type. The size, shape, and markings of the seeds of many plants have adaptive value in the dispersal of the plant, but none can be shown for the gourd, whose fruit appears to be the primary dispersal unit. One wonders whether, perhaps, although seeds were apparently not of extensive use to man, he did not practice deliberate selection for some reason.

Mature gourds will float, and it might appear that this type of fruit is an adaptation for dispersal by water. If it is adapted for water dispersal, we might expect it to be native to river banks or areas subject to periodic flooding, and indeed some of the relatives of the gourd do grow in such places; but some investigators have concluded that the bottle gourd is wild in grasslands or bushlands, which would hardly seem the ideal place for dispersal by water. Perhaps these investigators are incorrect, or perhaps its primary means of dispersal is not by water. There is also a second problem: how do the seeds get out of the thick walled gourd in nature?

Man, of course, has been caring for the bottle gourd for thousands of years so that the gourd no longer has to rely on nature for its propagation. Our present concern is with the wild type of the bottle gourd, and we are hampered by not knowing what the wild gourd was like, but we might suppose that it was very much like the cultivated plant in most features. Perhaps the fruit wall was not quite as thick as it is in the domesticated type. I do not take too seriously a colleague's suggestion that, since gourds grow in Africa, obviously the elephant is the dispersal agent, for the seeds are released when the gourd is stepped on. Sometimes gourds climb trees and in falling from a tall tree the fruit might break when it hits the ground, but probably as often as not the plants grow on the ground. I have observed in my own garden that a fruit left out over winter may have a hole gnawed in it by some rodent, apparently in a search for seeds. However, just as with my pollination observations, we don't know if this is true in the tropics. If indeed a gourd is dispersed by water, perhaps eventually it will crack against rocks and the seeds will be released.

By now it should be obvious that not much is known about the dispersal of gourds. It would be interesting to have some firsthand observations, for, as we shall see in ensuing chapters, the natural dispersal of gourds is of some concern in trying to explain the wide distribution of this plant in pre-historic times, unless we assume that man alone was responsible for its wide distribution, a notion that cannot be lightly dismissed.

In a previous paragraph it was mentioned that bottle gourds are native to Africa; this statement deserves some elaboration. This gourd is cultivated throughout much of the world today, and its original homeland has long been in some doubt. De Candolle in his *Origin of Cultivated Plants* pointed out that in seeking the place of nativity of a domesticated plant we look for that region in which it grows wild, but he realized that this is not always a simple matter, for sometimes domesticated plants may escape from cultivation and revert to a wild-type existence.

Very few botanists can ever study a widespread species throughout its entire range, but it is still possible to examine specimens collected from many parts of it. Specimens that botanists collect are pressed and dried. These dried specimens are mounted on paper and placed in repositories, called herbaria, in museums and universities, where they may be examined by others. I have examined a number of such specimens, particularly from the Americas, but, although the collector tells where the plant was collected, he often fails to indicate whether the specimen was found growing wild or in cultivation. Some specimens are labeled "escape," indicating that the collector thought that the plant had escaped from cultivation and was growing as a weed, but one wonders how the collector can be sure he has an escape and not a truly wild plant. In fact, I have seen gourds growing in places where they appeared to be wild, only to learn later that they were cultivated. A cultivated gourd requires little or no care, so it is not unlikely that some reportedly "wild" gourds may have actually been cultivated plants. There are several early reports from botanists that the plant grew wild in India and southeastern Asia, but in more recent works from this part of the world such statements are not seen. Does this mean that the earlier botanists were mistaken, or has the plant ceased to occur in the wild state? There are, however, recent reports from Africa that the species apparently grows wild there. The only conclusion that can be reached is that the gourd may still occur as a wild plant, but there is no certainty that it does. Thus, we can hardly use wild gourds to settle the question as to the original home of the bottle gourd.

N. I. Vavilov, the great Russian student of cultivated plants whose life ended in prison because he wouldn't recant his belief in "western genetics" in the face of Lysenko, maintained that the center of origin of a cultivated plant would generally be found in the area where it was most variable. The bottle gourd appears to have its greatest variability in Africa. We now know, however, that centers of variability may not always be centers of origin, so perhaps no particular significance should be attached to the great diversity among the bottle gourds of Africa as far as trying to determine the plant's place of origin.

Fossil remains of the bottle gourd might help establish the place of its origin, but unfortunately none has yet been reported. There is, however, an extensive archaeological record. The parts recovered are usually fragments of the rind, sometimes seeds, rarely whole gourds. Many of these archaeological specimens have been discovered only very recently.

There is an abundance of finds from the Americas; the oldest reported comes from the highlands near Ayacucho, Peru, dated at 13,000–11,000 B.C. There are many other reports from Peru, particularly from the coast, the oldest being dated at 6000–4000 B.C. A number have been reported from Mexico, the oldest coming from a level dated at 7000–5000 B.C. There are also several reports from both the southwestern and eastern United States, but these are all fairly recent, none going back before the first millenium B.C.

In the Old World, the earliest report by far comes from Spirit Cave in Thailand, dated between 10,000 and 6000 B.C. There are records from New Guinea at 350 B.C. and from various other parts of the Pacific in early Christian times. From Africa the gourd is reported from the Twelfth Dynasty

81

in Egypt, from Zambia, and from South Africa, all dating to around 2000 B.C. There are also later reports from Egypt and one from Kenya at around 900 B.C.

In evaluating these reports we have to consider both the identification and the dating. Most of the dates, with the exception of those from Egypt, have been figured by the radio-carbon method, and these are fairly reliable—give or take a few hundred years or so. It is comforting, of course, when there are several reports from an area that have been independently dated and give dates in close agreement. Thus, for both Peru and Mexico, it seems well established that gourds were there quite early, but for the earliest report from Peru, given as between 13,000 and 11,000 B.C., there may be some question. Some archaeologists have thought that perhaps the gourd was intrusive at this level and actually comes from a higher level that would place it around 6000 B.C.

As to the identity of the gourds, most of the American finds have been determined by Dr. Thomas Whitaker or by Dr. Hugh Cutler, or by both of those specialists in the family; and I think we can have considerable confidence in their identifications. Some of these, of course, could prove to be incorrect, but I think that more likely with some of the specimens from the Old World. The find from Thailand particularly raises some question. A few years ago I saw a photograph of a specimen of this material, and it appeared rather unlike any gourd known to me. Sometime later I was able to borrow specimens through the kindness of Douglas Yen of the Bishop Museum of Honolulu. The loan consisted of two small fragments of what could have been the rind of a gourd. One of these (No. 17) was excellently preserved. It measured 1.7 mm. in thickness; most gourds have rinds around 4 mm. thick, but I have one specimen from New Guinea only 2 mm. thick. So on the basis of thickness alone it seems unlikely that this specimen came from a gourd. The slight undulate surface of the specimen and the presence of an inner wall, which is lacking in the gourd, eliminated any possibility of its being a gourd. The second specimen (No. 53) posed greater problems, for it was charred. It was, however, 2.3 mm. thick, so it did fall within the size range of the gourd. In order to have comparative material, I broke three of my gourds and charred the fragments in a fireplace. Then I carefully broke a small piece from the archaeological specimen in order to have a fresh surface for comparison, and I did the same with my charred gourds. The specimens were studied under magnification (x 45) for several hours. The cellular nature of the archaeological specimens was quite different from that of my gourds. The cells of the latter were large and irregular, whereas those of the former appeared to be smaller and more regular. Moreover, the archaeological section showed a series of cavities, and I could only guess that these might be secretory structures in the original tissue. The modern specimens showed no such inclusions. It would, perhaps, be possible to make a more detailed study by making thin sections for microscopic examination, but I did not have the setup to do so; moreover, it would have meant sacrificing most of the archaeological specimen. I was satisfied, however, from my examination that the archaeological material did not come from a gourd, although I was at a loss to identify it. Thus, the Americas reserve the clear distinction of having the earliest known remains of the gourd.

Although it is fairly certain that the gourds found at all of the archaeological sites were used by man, it is not known whether they came from wild or cultivated plants. Cultivation of plants in the Americas probably began sometime around 6000 B.C., so it is possible that the gourds found after this date could have been cultivated, but not necessarily so.

The archaeological record is obviously incomplete. Some areas, such as the wet tropics, are not conducive to preservation of plant material; some areas have not been sampled at all and others, only inadequately. So the fact that the gourd has not been found archaeologically in certain regions must be interpreted with great caution. Nevertheless, attention should be called to some of the regions where they have not been found. There are no reports from the Near East, an area where there has been extensive archaeological investigation and where agriculture is known to have been practiced quite early. Wheat and barley were being cultivated there before 7000 B.C. Gourds are grown there today. Pottery remains resembling gourds have been found, and there is an Assyrian word for gourd, but this is not the kind of concrete evidence that the actual plant remains give. There is now beginning to be assembled a fair number of archaeological reports from both India and China, but the gourd is yet to be reported. There is a Sanskrit word for gourd, and from this and other lines of evidence we may suppose that the plant is fairly old in India. The gourd is mentioned as being used both as a vegetable and as a water container in four poems from China that go back to early in the first millenium. Thus, we may suppose that the gourd was introduced there earlier, but exactly when it reached both China and India must remain in doubt.

From the archaeological record one might be tempted to conclude that the gourd was indigenous to the Americas (Peru and/or Mexico) and went from there to Africa. It could, of course, be that the gourd had a relatively late entry into Africa, but in view of the incompleteness of the archaeological record it would be dangerous to draw such a conclusion from that record alone. It is apparent that we cannot use archaeological data to determine the homeland of the gourd, so we must turn to other lines of evidence.

Until very recently botanists had considered *Lagenaria* monotypic—that is, that there was only one species in the genus. Recent taxonomic studies, however, indicate that certain species previously placed in other genera actually should be assigned to *Lagenaria*. There are five of these species; all agree with the bottle gourd in many of their characteristics, particularly in having a pair of glands at the apex of the leaf stalk. Moreover, it has been possible to hybridize some of these species with the gourd, which also indicates a close relationship. All of these wild species are found in Africa, one extending into Madagascar. The fact that all of the relatives of the gourd are African indicates that the gourd itself might be native to Africa.

This is the best evidence presently available so far as I am concerned for considering the gourd native to Africa, and in the present work I shall assume that it is. This evidence is not absolutely conclusive, however, for sometimes not all species of a genus are native to the same continent or even the same hemisphere. It will be recalled that in *Luffa*, for example, two species are definitely American, whereas the remainder are native to the Old World. Very likely the genus *Lagenaria* had its origin in Africa, but it is still possible that the gourd originated in either the Americas or Asia from an ancestral species that migrated there early from Africa and is now extinct.

The wild African species deserve more attention. These do not have common names in English, so I shall have to use the scientific names. I have grown three of these species, *Lagenaria abyssinica*, *L. sphaerica*, and *L. brevifolia*. These wild species are all perennials, whereas the bottle gourd is an annual. *Lagenaria abyssinica* failed to flower in the three years I grew it, so I have nothing further to say about it. The other two flowered both in the greenhouse and in the field after placing out plants that had been started three months earlier in the greenhouse. Both species are rather ornamental, with more delicate leaves and flowers than those of the gourd. The flowers are open during the day and have a very pleasant aroma, which is entirely lacking in the bottle gourd. Both species are reported to bear their male and female flowers on separate plants, but I had a plant of *Lagenaria sphaerica* that produced both male and female flowers. However, all three of my plants of *L. brevifolia* produced only female flowers, so I had to pollinate them with pollen of the gourd in order to secure fruits. The fruits of both species are rather attractive, very dark green, streaked or mottled with white, and varying from the size of a baseball to that of a volley ball. I have some that I harvested over two years ago and they have scarcely faded at all. Their flesh is quite bitter.

I have seen no reports of the fruits of these wild species

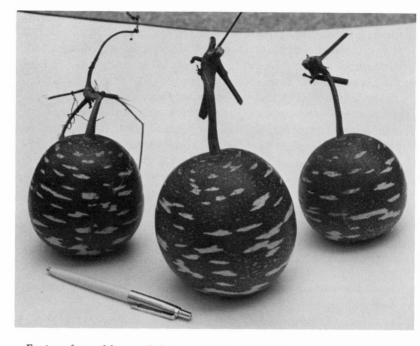

Fruits of a wild gourd *(Lagenaria brevifolia).*

having been used as utensils, probably because the fruit wall is much thinner and more fragile than that of the gourd. In parts of Africa, however, *Lagenaria brevifolia* is used in other ways. Water containing ashes and pieces of the fruit is used by tanners for dehairing hides. In the eastern Sudan the Arabs have been reported to chew the seeds while smoking tobacco to achieve a kind of intoxication, and the seeds have been used to stupefy fish.

The hybrids that I secured in crosses of the two wild species with the gourd gave rise to extremely vigorous plants. These plants were more or less intermediate between the parents for many characters and in others approached the condition found in the wild species. All of the plants produced only male flowers and these failed to produce pollen. Hybrids showing some degree of fertility, however, have been secured by others.

One other fact concerning *Lagenaria brevifolia* is of some interest. It has been reported as growing wild in Brazil. A collection was made at the turn of the century at Praia Grande in the state of Rio de Janiero. Whether the plant still grows there I have been unable to determine, but the recent development of beaches in this region may well have eliminated it. Nor have I seen any information on how the plant might have arrived there. Was it deliberately introduced by man? But why? Could it have become established in Brazil by fruits having floated across the Atlantic from Africa?

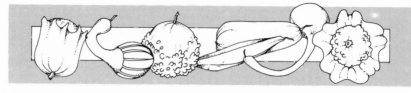

8.
A Personal Note

With the reader's indulgence, I should like to present a chapter on my background with gourds, for it will set the stage for some of the discussion that is to follow as well as present my credentials for such a discussion. It might also be of some interest. Some twenty-five years ago I started growing a few gourds in the Indiana University experimental gardens, along with the sunflowers and chili peppers that occupied most of my research time. I had no serious interest in the gourds at first, but they did furnish excellent flowers to use for my course in flowering plant taxonomy. Then a few years later when I began teaching a course in economic botany, I used the fruits to show to my class, and very shortly I found myself devoting a whole lecture to gourds. Two of my friends, Dr. Thomas Whitaker of the United States Department of Agriculture and Dr. Hugh Cutler of the Missouri Botanical Garden, were the foremost American authorities on gourds, and I followed their publications on the subject as they appeared. In 1965 when a former student of mine, Jack Humbles, returned to Indiana after having spent two years teaching in Tanzania, he brought seeds with him of some kind of gourd. He asked me what kind, but I couldn't tell him, for I

Seeds that started the author
on a study of gourds: above,
seeds from Tanzania; below,
"typical" seeds.

had never seen seeds like these before. All of the bottle gourds
that I had grown had a very different type of seed. Although
I was well aware that cultivated plants showed tremendous
variation, I didn't think that Humbles' seeds could have come
from the bottle gourd. After I grew them out, I discovered
that indeed the plant was a bottle gourd, but I still wondered
if it perhaps was a distinct species of *Lagenaria*.

I already knew that earlier botanists had described several
species of *Lagenaria*, and I was also well aware that botanists
in the last quarter of a century or so had generally agreed
that all of these named species actually belonged to the single
species, *Lagenaria siceraria*. I also knew that a Russian work-
er, Kobiakova, in 1930 after a rather detailed study of gourds
had concluded that, although the gourds of Africa and Asia
showed a number of differences, they still belonged to a single
species. I decided to have the paper translated so that I could
give it careful study, for by now I had decided that perhaps
the gourds needed more attention. This decision was later
strengthened when I read a paper by three eminent scientists,
Paul Mangelsdorf, a botanist, Scotty MacNeish, and Gordon
Willey, both anthropologists, who wrote, "The bottle gourd

more than any other species involved in tracing the origins of American agriculture needs the attention of taxonomists, geneticists and cytologists."

As I thought of the African seeds I had seen, I wondered if perhaps there was more than one species of bottle gourd, despite current opinion, and I resolved that I would look into the matter myself. Although I had plenty of research projects under way with other plants, I decided that I could manage to work gourds in somehow.

What I needed was a large sample of gourds from all around the world. Because it was out of the question for me to do all the collecting myself, I wrote letters requesting seed from botanists, anthropologists, agricultural officials, Peace Corps volunteers, missionaries, and former students of mine in various parts of the world. I did not receive answers to some of the letters, but this was not too surprising, perhaps, for I had never met many of the people to whom I was writing. I did, however, receive many replies, some of which contained seeds, as well as information on the local cultivation and use of gourds.*

After three years I had one hundred and eighty different collections from various parts of the world. I purposely avoided using seed from seed companies, because I had no way of knowing its original source. What I hoped to obtain was representatives of gourds that had been grown in a given country for a long time. Ideally I would have liked to have a picture of the gourd variation that existed before the great ocean voyages began in the last decade of the fifteenth century, following which there was a great exchange of plants from one part of the world to another. Obviously this was impossible, for I had no way of knowing how many of the collections I received might represent fairly recent introduc-

---

*One person replied that while he had an intimate knowledge of bottles, particularly those containing spirits, he was totally unaware of the whereabouts of the bottle gourd.

tions. In fact, I had written to a Peace Corps volunteer on one of the Pacific Islands, and he replied that the people on his island no longer grew gourds but that he was obtaining seeds from a seed company in the United States for the people to plant. If I had written to him a year or two later, I might have obtained seeds that could have given some unaccountable results in my study of the geographical variation in gourds.

The plants from the collected seed were grown in the garden, and detailed measurements were made on the seeds, flowers, leaves, and fruits. I also made crosses between the different kinds of gourds and between those from different continents. I obtained good seed from all of the fifty-three hybridizations I attempted, most of them on the first try. All of the hybrid seed that was then grown gave vigorous plants, largely intermediate between their parents in most characters, as would be expected, and all of them were fertile. I even grew a second generation from some of the hybrids, and they showed the kind of segregation of the parental characters as would be expected, and they, too, were fertile.

The results of the hybridizations certainly suggested that only a single species was involved. A species is sometimes defined as a group of organisms able to exchange genes freely among themselves but not with other such groups. There are some exceptions to this, of course, and a number of perfectly good plant species are able to hybridize freely in the garden, but do not do so in nature. However, I didn't feel that the gourd was one of the exceptions, and the morphological studies of the leaves, flowers, and seeds largely confirmed my impression.

There is no need here to go into the details concerning the morphological variation, for these data have been published elsewhere. There was a lot of variability shown in many characteristics of the plants in addition to those of the fruits, but there were no clear-cut demarcations indicating that more than a single species was involved. My observations did confirm and extend those of Kobiakova. Two major geographical

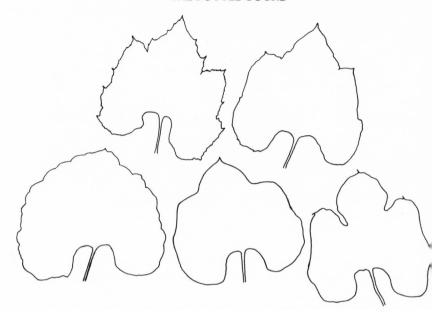

Leaves of bottle gourds: above, from Asia; below, from the Americas.

races, or subspecies, could be recognized—one comprising all the samples from Asia and the other, those from Africa and the Americas.

The plants of the latter group, which are known formally as *Lagenaria siceraria* subspecies *siceraria*, have leaves generally with smooth or ruffled margins, unlobed or rounded-lobed; flowers small to medium-sized; sepals or calyx lobes short and broad; and seeds usually dark in color and less than twice as long as broad. The Asiatic gourds, *Lagenaria siceraria* subspecies *asiatica*, on the other hand, have leaves that are somewhat saw-toothed on the margins and sharply three- to five-lobed; larger flowers with long, slender calyx lobes; and light-colored seeds that are usually more than twice as long as broad.

There were a few collections that did not exactly fit into the subspecies expected on the basis of their geographical location. For example, a collection from Trinidad showed several characteristics rather typical of Asiatic gourds (for seed, see page 96); but when it is realized that this island has a large population of Asiatic Indians who could well have brought gourds with them, we have a possible explanation for the discrepancy. Some of the gourds from Arizona were also somewhat atypical for American gourds. Perhaps these represent not original races of this plant but recent purchases from seed companies, whose seeds, of course, could have come from almost anywhere in the world.

Although my one hundred and eighty collections were a very small sample of this wide-ranging species, I felt that the results were of some interest. Since the original study was completed, I have grown over two hundred additional accessions, and a study of them bore out my previous conclusions with very few exceptions. I was particularly disappointed, however, that I did not have more material from the Pacific region. For the original study I had gourds only from the Caroline Islands and the Philippines. Since that time I have grown material from Niue, New Guinea, and New Zealand. All of these gourds are referable to the Asiatic race, except those from New Guinea, which constitute a special problem and are treated in a later chapter. Unfortunately, only two of the samples come from Polynesia. The fact that more material was not secured is hardly surprising, for E. S. Dodge in 1943 wrote:

After serving its period of usefulness to man, the gourd, as a culturally important element in Polynesia, is no more. Except for specimens in museums, — gone are the *hula* drums, the lover's whistles, and the "Niihau calabashes." No more do the Maori feast on roasted pigeons taken from their own fat in the great preserving gourds. We look at an object in a case and strain the imagination to see it in its own setting. But as year swiftly follows year, the once living culture of the primitive people of old recedes farther from the objects which it created into the background of antiquity.

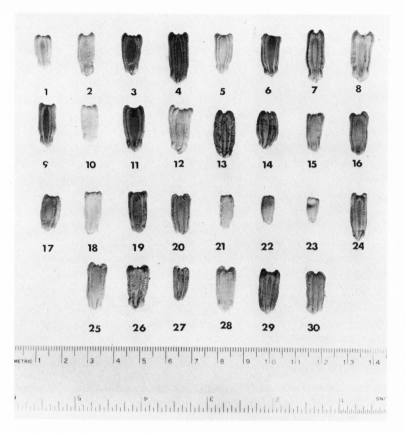

Seeds of bottle gourds from Asia. 1–16, India; 17, Thailand; 18–19, Pakistan; 20, Malaysia; 21–25, Japan; 26–27, Philippines; 28, Caroline Island; 29, Hawaii; 30, Malaysia (× 7/10).

Seeds of bottle gourds from Africa. 1–15, Tanzania; 16, Egypt; 17–29, Ghana; 30–31, Uganda; 32–36, South Africa; 37, Nigeria (× 7/10).

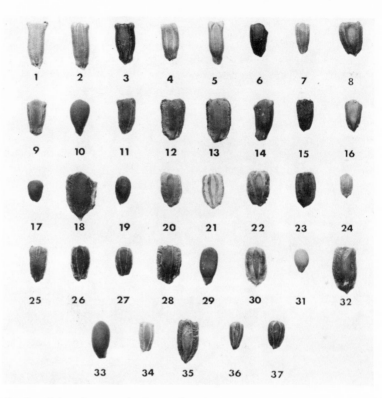

Seeds of bottle gourds from the Americas. 1–5, Arizona; 6–17, Mexico; 18–19, Costa Rica; 20–22, Trinidad; 23, Colombia; 24–25, Ecuador; 26–29, Peru; 30–36, Brazil; 37, Argentina ($\times$ 7/10).

The Polynesian area is of interest because there were claims, particularly before the gourd was known to be so ancient in Peru, that it went from Polynesia to South America; others, however, saw it going to Polynesia from South America. Thor Heyerdahl is among the latter. In his *American Indian in the Pacific* in 1952, as well as in more recent works, he maintains that Polynesia was originally settled from South America, using the presence of the gourd in Polynesia as some of the evidence for this theory. It must be admitted that there is one plant, the sweet potato, that is generally accepted as having been introduced into the Pacific area from South America in prehistoric times, and it is most likely that it was carried there by man. All of the other food and other useful plants of Polynesia, however, were derived from southeastern Asia or are native to the Pacific region. Most scholars are of the opinion that Polynesia was settled by people coming from the west, and that, although there could have been voyages to or from the Americas in prehistoric times, these had little effect on the culture of the islands.

Heyerdahl discusses, and then dismisses, the possibility that the gourd might have floated to Polynesia. I do not feel that such a hypothesis is out of the question, however, although I think it more likely that the gourd was carried into the Pacific by man from southeastern Asia, where it is probably a fairly old plant. My two samples of the gourd from Niue and New Zealand are nearest to the Asian race; while this sample is much too small to draw any firm conclusions, it is all we have to go on at the moment. Perhaps future archaeological work will give more evidence.

While my study has thus far told us very little about the gourds of Polynesia, it has shown that the gourds of Africa and America are very similar. Thus, I think we must look for an explanation as to how the gourd crossed the Atlantic in prehistoric times, and this I shall develop in the next two chapters.

Gourd used to hold fish in Ghana. (Courtesy of FAO.)

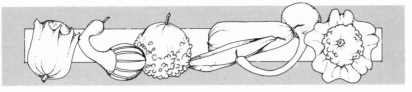

9.
Gourds across the Ocean, I

Cultural Diffusion versus Independent Invention

If the gourd is native to Africa, as many suppose, then how did it reach the Americas several thousand years ago? There are two main schools of thought on the matter, but, before getting into these, several other possibilities must be eliminated.

First, it must be pointed out that it is extremely unlikely, if not absolutely impossible, that the species *Lagenaria siceraria* could have originated more than once. In fact, virtually all species have had but a single origin, the only possible exceptions known to me being a few polyploid species which could have originated by hybridization of two species followed by chromosome doubling. Such an event could have occurred in two separate areas. The gourd, however, is not a polyploid species.

It is thought that the first Americans came from Asia across the Bering Strait. How long ago this took place is not agreed upon—30,000 years ago or even much earlier. There is no need to go into details here, for so far as I know no one has ever suggested that the gourd entered the Americas by this route. Even if these early migrants, say, had somehow acquired the gourd in Asia, it is unlikely that they could have reached a place in the Americas where the gourd could have

Household gourds in Dahomey. (Courtesy of FAO.)

grown before the seeds had lost their viability. Moreover, these early migrations were by people who did not know agriculture and probably brought very little with them in the way of cultural baggage.

It is now generally agreed that at one time Africa and South America were a single continent and that they have gradually drifted apart to occupy their present positions. So one might postulate that the gourd was already present in both parts of what in time was to become the two separate continents. The difficulty with such a hypothesis is that present evidence indicates that the separation of the continents began before the flowering plants came into existence or at a time when only a few primitive families of flowering plants were known. The cucurbits are not one of these primitive families.

Thus we are left with two possibilities—the gourd floated across the ocean or it was carried by man. The former hypothesis received considerable support in 1954 when Thomas W. Whitaker and George F. Carter demonstrated that gourds could float in sea water for at least 347 days—ample time to have crossed the Atlantic by floating—and that the seeds still retained viability. In fact, these scientists found that the seeds would still germinate after having remained in these gourds for six years. However, as they point out, the fact that the gourd could have floated across the ocean does not mean that it did. In this connection, the often quoted statement of the noted geographer Carl O. Sauer deserves repeating: The gourd "is a cultigen as we know it in America and depends upon man for its preservation. It is in no sense a strand or marsh plant. The theory of its accidental dissemination involves, in addition to the undamaged transit of an ocean, a waiting agriculturist who carried it from the seashore to a suitable spot for cultivation."

In spite of this statement a large number of people believe that the gourd must have floated across the ocean. Many others, on the contrary, feel that it must have been introduced by man. To tally up the numbers who hold one or the other of these views might be interesting, but it would solve nothing. To understand better the two schools of thought, some background into cultural diffusion versus independent invention may be helpful. In the field of anthropology few theories have provoked more heated discussions than transoceanic contact before Columbus. Not only will some discussion on this subject prove useful in trying to understand the movements of the gourd but also later when we come to its various uses, which show a remarkable parallel development in widely scattered parts of the world.

There are indeed many parallels in the development of civilization in the Old World and the New—the uses of metal, writing, agricultural systems, religions, and political organizations. There are also some exact or almost exact similarities, as, for example, in the blowguns of Indonesia and the Amazon Basin. The extreme independent inventionists would have all of the civilization of the New World arise without any influences from the Old, the similarities to be explained as basic human responses to similar conditions; whereas the extreme diffusionists would have all of the New World civilization developing as the result of contacts with the Old World. In the early part of this century, in particular, there were many who tried to explain all of the New World culture as coming from the Old, some even going so far as to derive it from the Lost Tribes of Israel. Perhaps somewhat as a reaction to those extremists, others soon claimed that there had been no contacts between the Old World and the New before Columbus. Today, even with far more archaeological material available and with more accurate dating, the controversy shows little sign of abating. The proof that the diffusionists offer is not accepted by the independent inventionists, and, in reply, the diffusionists maintain that the kind of proof that the other side demands can never be forthcoming.

Let us consider the origin of agriculture, for example—one of the few cultural traits that I am qualified to discuss. According to the archaeological record, agriculture had its beginnings in the Near East around ten thousand years ago, and some two thousand years later in the Americas. The plants cultivated in the Old World were entirely different from those cultivated in the Americas, but this alone doesn't mean that agriculture in the latter area did not come from the Old World. In a long ocean voyage, perhaps an accidental one, it would not be surprising if no seeds survived the journey, but the *idea* of planting could have. Probably the majority of those concerned with the subject, however, feel that agriculture had completely separate origins in the Old World and the New. In fact, some feel that agriculture arose independently in several different places both in the Old World and the New.

The failure of the wheel to be utilized in the Americas is often cited as evidence against prehistoric contacts between the Old World and the New, but it is hardly decisive; wheeled toys were known in Mexico. Moreover, there were several domesticated animals available for pulling wheeled vehicles in the Old World, whereas there were no such animals, unless one would include such unlikely ones as the dog and the llama, for such kinds of transport in the New World.

That there were contacts across the oceans before Columbus is now fairly widely accepted, but the question remains whether they had any impact on the culture of the New World. Those voyages in the few centuries immediately preceding Columbus' voyage perhaps would have been too late to be of great significance. If voyages took place several thousand years ago, which must remain a possibility, the question may also be raised as to whether they had any impact. If a small boatload of people arrived in the Americas from across the sea, perhaps they were all eaten by their hosts.

I find this all a most intriguing problem, perhaps largely because we still have so few answers. Perhaps I should explain my own position. I do not think I have any preconceived ideas in regard to transoceanic diffusion before Columbus. In fact, I have sometimes been criticized for straddling the fence. Two of my teachers were Carl O. Sauer and Edgar Anderson, neither of whom could be called an anti-diffusionist. I will say, however, that at times I have felt that some of the diffusionists in attempting to use botanical materials to support their claims have been most unscientific. Secondly, I must admit that at one time I found it hard to believe that a simple idea could not have occurred independently in two or more places, for, if not, it meant that man was not a terribly intelligent animal. But in recent years, from having worked with administrative officials in a university from departmental chairman on up, I am beginning to think that perhaps he isn't.

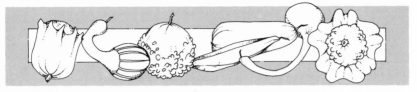

10.
Gourds across the Ocean, II

Our Mother, the Gourd

Many people become enthusiastic about gourds, but few can equal Donald Lathrap, an anthropologist at the University of Illinois, when it comes to discussing their significance in early agriculture. I have followed his works with great interest, and, although I do not always agree with his botanical interpretations, I find them most stimulating.

One of his papers which provides the most recent attempt to account for the presence of the gourd in the Americas certainly requires some discussion. Before turning to that one, however, I would like to refer to an earlier paper of his, entitled "Gifts of the Cayman: Some Thoughts on the Subsistence Basis of Chavín." Chavín, an early culture of South America, apparently had considerable influence on the later cultures in Peru, and perhaps even Mexico as well. At Chavín de Huantar in Peru, a carved granite shaft was found. It is now on display in a museum in Lima and is referred to as the Obelisk Tello. Thought to date to around 1000 B.C., it is considered one of the most "richly conceived and elaborately executed" examples of Chavín art. It probably served as an idol and direct representation of a deity, a cayman. It is not this major deity that concerns us here, however, but certain other representations that are thought to portray plants. Identification of these would presumably provide us with knowledge of the plants that were the most important to these people, for, as Lathrap points out, the inhabitants of Chavín were so inconsiderate as to leave us no actual plant remains. Identification of prehistoric, and sometimes historic as well, religious art motifs is not always a simple matter. An examination of the drawings will make this point clear.

Figure 1 Lathrap interprets as manioc, or cassava, a very basic food plant of tropical America, but which many readers may know only in the form of tapioca. His argument is convincing and I accept his identification. Figure 2 shows a plant on top of a jaguar's head; he identifies this tentatively as achira, *Canna edulis*, which is rather similar to our garden cannas. He thinks it is very unlikely that it could be maize, and I agree with him. It could be the achira, but I would also suggest the possibility of tobacco, and the botanist Barbara Pickersgill has suggested pineapple. The plant in Figure 3 he identifies as a chili pepper and feels that it is from a cultivated plant. I feel, however, that the size of the fruit in relation to the size of the flower (lower left), might indicate that it is a wild plant. But more than that, I find the corolla very disturbing, for it is a type that is rare in peppers, being found only in the *ulipica* of Bolivia. In fact, the corolla could well be that of tobacco, although the fruit is a good representation of a pepper. Could we have two plants represented here? Lathrap originally identified the plant in Figure 4 as cotton, but, after Pickersgill called attention to the similarity of the object in the lower right with that of the fruit of a gourd, he changed his mind, and wrote:

Once this [object] is identified, as it must be, with the matured and dried fruit of . . . the bottle gourd, all other problems disappear; the leaves and the distinction between male and female flowers are remarkably accurate for that species. Particularly well observed is the long, jagged calyx of the closed flower in the upper left.

Indeed, the structure in the lower right could be a fruit of a

Indian representations of plants; 1–4 from the Obelisk Tello (from Lathrap, 1973), 5 from Cuna Indian mola (redrawn from Eleanor Moore, *Gourd Seed*, Vol. XXXI, No. 2 [1970]). 1, manioc; 2, achira (?); 3, chili pepper (?); 4, gourd (?); 5, gourd.

gourd, but I disagree with practically everything else he has to say, for the calyx in the gourd is much shorter than the corolla, the corolla has five lobes, and I can't make out any distinction in the sex of the flowers in the drawing. Originally, therefore, I could not accept it as a gourd, and I tried to think of something better to offer. Sweet potato or squash, perhaps, but both of these would raise as many problems as did the gourd. Perhaps it was a composite of several plants. I forgot about the problem until I was paging through some old issues of *The Gourd Seed*, where I saw a photograph of a design (Figure 5) in a mola from the Cuna Indians of Panama. In the article the design was identified as a gourd, and I find it acceptable. I also find certain similarities of this design with the supposed gourd of the obelisk, so perhaps the latter is indeed a gourd.

If the plant depicted by the Chavín artist is a gourd, it may well represent the earliest artistic representation of this plant. Even if it is not a gourd, there is enough other evidence to indicate that the gourd was a most important plant to the ancient inhabitants of the Americas, as we shall shortly learn.

Lathrap's second paper was the result of a conference devoted to the subject of the origin of agriculture, which had been organized by Charles Reed and held in Chicago in 1973. Lathrap's paper bears the marvelous title, "Our Father the Cayman, Our Mother the Gourd: Spinden Revisited, or a Universal Model for the Emergence of Agriculture in the New World." The cayman has already been introduced, and perhaps it should be pointed out that H. J. Spinden was an anthropologist who in 1915 presented his ideas on the origin of agriculture. To consider Lathrap's paper in its entirety is beyond the scope of this book, so I shall largely confine my remarks to his treatment of gourds, without, however, repeating such material as has already been presented in earlier chapters.

After reviewing the importance of the gourd to man, he mentions its frequent occurrences in creation myths from various parts of the world. From this he concludes that to early people the gourd was the universal womb or the whole universe. Moreover, he maintains that the gourd as a cultivated plant provided the womb in which more elaborate agricultural systems evolved, or, more precisely, that "the artificial propagation of the bottle gourd and certain technologically significant crops as cotton and fish poisons imposed particular disciplines upon man and in the context of these behavioral patterns all the other nutritionally significant agricultural systems arose."

He accepts an African origin for the gourd, and he maintains that its survival in other places depends on human intervention, pointing out that there is evidence in southeastern Asia that, when a cultivated area is allowed to return to a wild state, the gourd is one of the first plants to disappear. A recent introduction into the Americas is suggested, because the typical insects of squash, an American cucurbit, avoid the bottle gourd, which is most commonly attacked by an Old World insect, the melon aphid. The foregoing considerations and the archaeological record lead him to the conclusion that the gourd was domesticated in Africa at a very early time and reached America and Asia as a fully domesticated plant. In answer to those who have maintained that the gourd once grew wild in America and Asia, he asks why then has it disappeared completely from both areas. "Repeated and intensive search" for wild gourds, he states, has been fruitless.

He goes on at some length to develop the thesis that agriculture could have been practiced, at least in a primitive way, in Africa before 14,000 B.C., for obviously it would have to have been if the gourd reached Peru as a cultivated plant before 10,000 B.C. He points out that fishermen, who were largely sedentary people, would have been present in Africa. Their need for fish poison, gourds for fish-net floats, and cotton for making the nets might have led to the cultivation of these plants. This was probably originally done by transplanting the plants to the yards of their habitations. Eventually the gourd would be so modified and improved that it would no longer compete in the wild.

From Africa he would have the gourd arrive in northeastern Brazil, which seems the most likely place for it to enter South America; he feels that the diversity in the gourd in northeastern Brazil is compatible with the idea that it is ancient there. There is agreement, he believes, that it was a gourd net float that made the trip across the Atlantic. Such a gourd would not perpetuate itself because it is not a strand plant; therefore, once it arrived in Brazil (1) it could have been picked up by a man who knew of agriculture, recognized its usefulness, and took it home and planted its seeds; (2) or it could have been picked up by a genius, who, without any previous knowledge of agriculture, shouted "Eureka," and proceeded to plant the seed; or (3) a boatload of fishermen who made the transatlantic journey brought the gourd with them, and also likely carried cotton and fish-poison plants, which they introduced along with the gourd and a number of other cultural traits. After considering these three possibilities, he eliminates the first two and makes a "most reluctant" acceptance of the third.

He goes on to say the gourd would flourish on man's trash heaps about his villages, and thus the plant could be maintained. Gourds could have been carried from one area to another, perhaps as rattles (an idea he credits to me), and then after being accidentally broken they would be relegated to the dump heap, where more gourds would then spring up from the seeds. By such means the gourd would eventually have reached both Peru and Mexico. Moreover, it was the gourd, "our mother," that was directly responsible for the development of agriculture in the Americas.

In my summary of Lathrap's very long discussion, I may have done violence to some of his ideas, but not intentionally so. He has presented a most interesting hypothesis. It may be correct, but I see no way in which it can be proved or dis-

Gourds used in the Argungu Fishing Festival, near Sokoto, Nigeria.
(Photograph by Raymond W. Konan, courtesy of Mildred Konan.)

proved, at least with the evidence presently available. However, certain points require discussion.

I, too, accept Africa as the likely original home of the gourd, although, as I have indicated earlier, I do not think that assumption rests on a very firm foundation. Lathrap's attempt to use the presence of the melon aphid, an Old World species, on the gourds in America means little by itself. In fact, from observations in my garden I find that the spotted and striped cucumber beetles, both insects native to the Americas, are much more common pests.

Lathrap does not claim to be an authority on agriculture in Africa, and I am certainly not. The archaeological record I know, however, indicates that agriculture is fairly recent in western Africa, in the order of a few thousand years at the most. The archaeological record, as has already been mentioned, is incomplete, but there is no evidence at all of an early high culture in western Africa that might indicate that agriculture had developed there. Africans may well have been practicing a primitive type of agriculture for 14,000 years, but so may have the Americans. I feel that if African sailors did visit the Americas at the time postulated by Lathrap, they would have to have been carrying wild, not cultivated, gourds.

If it could be shown that other plants used by man were also introduced to America from Africa—Lathrap mentions the possibility of cotton and fish poisons—then his case would be strong indeed. The cotton story is very complicated, but there is the possibility that a wild species of cotton was introduced from Africa to the Americas, where it hybridized with a native species to produce the species ancestral to the American domesticated cottons. When, where, and how this happened is still a subject of disagreement, but botanists are now inclined to believe that man was in no way involved in the transfer. It has not been clearly shown that the plants used for fish poisons on either side of the Atlantic are the same species, and nothing more can be said until we have a better understanding of the taxonomy of these species. Lathrap also postulates the bringing in of other cultural traits, which brings us right back to the whole problem of cultural diffusion versus independent invention. I believe that some of the traits now found among Indians in the Amazon Basin have been postulated as having come across the Pacific rather than the Atlantic by some diffusionists.

That a gourd soon disappears from a cultivated area, once cultivation is abandoned, is probably not unlikely. Gourds are dependent upon disturbed areas, either as cultivated plants or as escapes, for their survival. Such disturbed areas today are usually created by man, but natural disturbances such as river flooding, forest fires started by lightning, earthquakes, and landslides do occur without man's aid. It is tempting to suggest that the gourd was originally a plant of naturally disturbed areas, perhaps along river banks, which would also explain why it has a fruit seemingly adapted for dispersal by water. Then, when man appeared on the scene and disturbed the environment by making villages, perhaps the gourd moved in with man. Thus, the gourd would have adopted man just as much as man did the gourd. Man has made it a domesticated plant, but even so it does not require the pampering that many of our domesticates do. In many places the plants are given no cultivation after the seeds are started. In this connection it is perhaps pertinent to mention that the Indians of Virginia believed that it was unlucky to plant gourds, so they simply scattered seeds on the ground to start new plantings.

Lathrap asks: if the gourd were once wild in the Americas and Asia, then why has it disappeared so completely from these areas? The same question might be asked for Africa, for it is far from certain that it grows wild there. Could it be that it has disappeared as a wild plant because it grew in the very same kinds of places that man chose for his habitations? If plants are found growing without man's aid in such places today, we tend to regard them as escapes rather than as truly wild plants. In spite of Lathrap's statement, I do not think that there has ever been an intensive and detailed search for a wild gourd in a great many areas. In fact, outside of

Barbara Pickersgill's work in northeastern Brazil, I know of no such search.

In the last thirty years increasing effort has led to the identification of the wild ancestors of many of our cultivated plants, but there are still some whose wild types are not known. Interestingly, among these are the wild ancestors of several of our squashes and pumpkins, which are clearly of American origin and have received more study than the gourd because of their greater economic importance.

I do not attach as much significance to the great variability of gourds in Brazil as Lathrap does. Although I feel that the gourd is quite ancient there, I do not think that the variability necessarily indicates great antiquity. Gourds are probably as variable in Peru and Mexico as they are in Brazil, and for many areas we have no information on the variability of gourds.

I could devote more comment to certain of Lathrap's statements, but the time has come for an alternative hypothesis. Very simply it is this—the gourd floated to America. This could have happened fifty thousand or a hundred thousand years ago, or even earlier, which would mean that it arrived in the Americas long before man did. Or it could have floated across more recently and have been discovered by man. I do not feel that it had to be a fish-net gourd that made the trip, but very well could have been a gourd that floated down a river to the ocean. Moreover, I do not necessarily feel that this happened only once. In fact, the many parallel variations in African and American gourds might be most readily explained by assuming multiple introductions. Parallel mutations after a single introduction, of course, are not out of the question. Not only do I think a gourd landed on the coast of Brazil, but I think it is also possible that one could have floated to Mexico. I am not, of course, denying any transatlantic crossings by man in prehistoric times, although I would think that any such voyages were later than Lathrap supposes. I do not even deny that these people could have brought gourds with them, but if they did they found them already in use in the Americas.

Such a hypothesis of long-distance dispersal by natural means might have caused raised eyebrows among past generations of botanists, who were trying to explain all discontinuous distributions across oceans by means of hypothetical land bridges or lost continents. Today, however, it is widely accepted that there are many examples of long-distance dispersal of plants by birds, wind, or water currents and subsequent establishment in the New World. After all, it has been shown that the gourd will float in salt water for a long period of time and that the seeds still remain viable, so the hypothesis I have adopted is hardly novel.

The gourd is certainly not the only plant that is common to both Africa and the Americas. The botanist Robert Thorne has tabulated one hundred and eight species, only twenty of which have had a long association with man, that are found in both tropical West Africa and tropical America. Some of these species are most likely dispersed by water, others by birds, and he concludes that long-distance dispersal by one or the other of these agents is the most likely explanation for the presence of these species on both sides of the Atlantic.

What would be the fate of a gourd if it washed up on the shores of America? Much to do has been made of the fact that it is not a strand plant—that is, it is not found as a member of shore communities of plants—but I don't think this necessarily proves that it could never become established on a beach. In fact, there is at least one firm record of it growing in such a site. The botanist Henri Pittier collected a specimen, now in the United States National Herbarium (4138), growing along a beach at Viento Frio in Panama. I am not claiming that this plant resulted from a transoceanic voyage, only that it proves it will grow upon a beach. Moreover, I am not sure it is necessary to prove this, for strong waves, perhaps the result of a hurricane, might carry gourds inland to a suitable site for growth.

So I claim it is likely that a gourd, probably wild, became established in the Americas after floating across the ocean. Only a single plant would be necessary, for self-pollination could produce more gourds. Perhaps it would have spread naturally from Brazil to reach both Peru and Mexico, but it seems more likely that man discovered a gourd on the coast, either a newly arrived one or one on a plant that had become established on or near a beach. This man would not necessarily have to be Sauer's "waiting agriculturist" or Lathrap's "genius," for the gourd could have been carried to his habitation and its seeds have given rise to plants in disturbed areas without any effort on his part. As the gourd came to be used by man, it would travel with him to new places, become a trade item, and spread over much of the Americas. Thus, there is no real need to postulate the existence of a wild gourd being found outside of man's habitations at any time in the Americas. Lathrap and I are largely in agreement as to the spread of the gourd in the Americas, but I would have it originally spread as a weed* rather than as a domesticated plant. We are also in agreement that more study of gourds is needed.

So I will propose a research project. I will go to western Africa. There I will buy gourds of various kinds. These will be pyroengraved with identifying marks and then released in the ocean. After a suitable interval I will go to Brazil to await the arrival of these gourds. After careful deliberation I have decided that I will spend my time at the beaches of

---

*What is a weed? Many definitions of weeds have been proposed—"a plant out of place," "a plant whose virtues have yet to be discovered," "a useless, unwanted plant" among them—but a definition that has gained more acceptance is that a weed is a plant that grows in disturbed places. In 1949 I defined a weed "as a plant that grows in places in some way disturbed by man or his domesticated animals" ("Enigma of the Weeds," *Frontiers*, Vol. XIII, No. 5). I think I might emend that definition today to allow weeds to occur in naturally disturbed areas as well.

Rio de Janiero, where I understand the scenery is very good; and I will hire assistants to comb the beaches farther north. I estimate that a grant of $100,000 would get the project underway; and if one of my gourds from Africa should arrive the first year, this amount might be sufficient. This proposal has not yet been submitted to any of the granting agencies, but I am prepared to listen to offers.

If a gourd should not arrive in Brazil, it does not, of course, necessarily destroy my hypothesis, for obviously such an event would have to happen only once. Nor if a gourd does arrive does it necessarily constitute proof of my hypothesis, but it should go a long way in helping it gain acceptance. Once this is accomplished, I shall propose a search for a wild gourd, although I would hesitate to do so in these troubled economic times; it would require a lot of money and take many years, for obviously I would have to visit many places not only in Africa but in the Americas and Asia as well. I also am somewhat reluctant to submit such a proposal, for I fear that the granting agencies might consider it nothing more than a wild gourd chase.

Now perhaps the reader understands why this book should have been called "Out of My Gourd."

A noble Indian woman of Pomeiock with a gourd container. From a drawing by John White in Theodore de Bry's *A Brief and True Report of the New Found Land of Virginia* (1590).

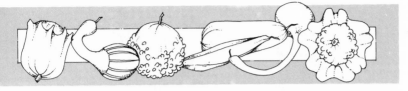

11.
Uses: General

The number of uses to which the gourd has been put is rather astounding. Dodge, for example, lists over forty different ways in which the ancient Hawaiians used the gourd. The list of uses that will be given here, I am sure, is very incomplete. I learn new ones all the time. For example, just the other day one of our students, Michele Jack, brought in some dye, or rocker, stamps made of gourd rind. These are used for imprinting designs on cloth in Nigeria, and she had obtained them when she was a Peace Corps volunteer there. In this chapter I shall take up the more common uses as well as some of the minor and rather unusual ones, and I shall reserve other chapters for certain special uses. It will be shown that gourds were used in many of the same ways in various parts of the world; without much doubt many of these uses go back thousands of years. Whether these similar uses in widely separated parts of the world result from independent invention or from cultural diffusion, I shall largely let the reader decide.

Containers

Probably the greatest use, and likely the first, has been as

Dipper gourd being used in Malawi. (Courtesy of FAO.)

containers; although they have been largely replaced for this purpose by glass, tin, and plastic, it is still their principal use in many tropical areas. There would be little point in attempting to list all of the things that the gourd was used to contain, as some authors have, but the more important ones deserve notice. The gourd makes an ideal receptacle for water. Some gourds come with an hour-glass figure, more or less, which made it easy to attach a rope for carrying them. When this type of gourd was not available, people

120

Gourd used to hold fertilizer in Nigeria. The fertilizer is being applied to a manioc plant. (Courtesy of FAO.)

Large gourds are used in parts of Mexico to collect the juice, or *agua miel* ("honey water"), from the Agave plant. The juice is then made into a beer. (Courtesy of Abraham D. Krikorian.)

Gourds used as containers for manioc, Sierra Leone. (Courtesy of FAO.)

Gourds used as beverage containers and cups in Ghana. (Courtesy of Ghana Information Services.)

found that, by tying a string around a gourd at an early stage of its growth, a constriction could be produced so that a rope could later be tied around it for carrying. The gourd served to cool the water by evaporation, just as an earthenware jar does, and for this reason continues to serve as a preferred receptacle for water as well as other liquids in many parts of the world. Some Indians in the southeastern United States claimed that the best drinking water always came from a gourd. It also served as a receptacle for milk in the United States, as it still does in parts of Africa, as well as the container for making butter and cheese. The Masais of Africa use gourds to collect blood when they bleed their cattle, and then drink the blood after adding salt to it. Halves of extremely large gourds serve as receptacles for making beer from bananas in Africa and from manioc in South America. Lime is used in connection with coca chewing in South America and the chewing of betel in Melanesia; in both regions very small gourds serve as lime pots.

Gourds were used to store grain and other solid foods, and also served as measures for grain. A large gourd placed upon a three-legged stand was used to preserve small birds for food among the Maoris of New Zealand. The Chokwes' of northeastern Angola similarly used them for storing ants, one of their delicacies. After the wings were removed, the ants were placed in the gourd with layers of salt, and hot water was added, after which the gourd was tightly stoppered until the ants were required for food.

Eating utensils such as plates, cups, dippers, and spoons were made from gourds in many places.

A favorite gourd when it was cracked or broken was not discarded but was repaired by sewing. This practice was found in such widely scattered places as Africa, South America, and Hawaii. I thought this would be extremely difficult, but I decided to try it myself, and found it rather easy. However, I had the advantage of steel needles, which were, of course, not available to some of the people who sewed gourds.

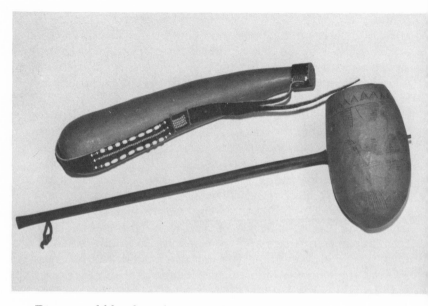

Dipper and blood-catching gourd from Tanzania.

After the invention of pottery, clay pots were used as containers, taking over some of the roles of gourds. The latter, however, continued to be used for many purposes. Being lighter than pots, gourds were preferred as containers for traveling. Some have thought that man's first pottery was based on gourds. Whether or not this is true, it is clear that gourds served as models for pottery in some places, as is most clearly evident from Lathrap's discoveries in Ecuador. It has been suggested that basketmaking began with the weaving of nets, and that nets were invented in order to have an easy way of carrying gourds. Certainly there are many early examples of pottery in the shape of gourds, and nets have been widely employed for carrying gourds, although this, of course,

Japanese water or wine gourd.

does not prove that pottery and weaving arose in the manner suggested. Nets may well have been first used for fishing.

Food

In an article on food plants of Middle America, three eminent scientists state that the gourd is inedible, and some anthropologists have expressed surprise that a nonfood plant should be one of man's first cultivated plants. They are mistaken, for the gourd was widely grown and much appreciated as a food plant. Moreover, there are plants—cotton, for example—that were useful to man for purposes other than food which were brought into domestication quite early, and it

127

may well be that the gourd was first cultivated for its importance as a receptacle and that its use as food was secondary. It is not unlikely, of course, that the first gourds cultivated were bitter, and that nonbitter mutants appeared after cultivation. Only the nonbitter kinds are used for food; today some of these are grown solely for use as food.

As a food plant today the gourd is apparently of greatest importance in China, Japan, and India, although it is also used for food in many tropical countries. I have seen the fruits for sale in many markets in Latin America. It is, however, hardly a major source of food in any of these countries. The fruits are cooked and eaten much as summer squash, or added as an ingredient to other dishes, such as curries. Although the natives apparently find the taste delicious, most Britons and Americans who have written of them have found them rather insipid.

In Japan the gourd flesh is cut into strips and placed in the sun to dry, or dried in specially constructed buildings, to preserve it for future use. Dried gourd shavings or strips may be found in some stores in this country under the name *Kanpyo*. The package informs us that the strips should be placed in boiling water and then rinsed before using. Recipes for preparing various dishes are also given on the label, but some knowledge of Japanese food is necessary for their use; for example, to make *chirashizuski*, "cut Kanpyo into 1/2 inch length. Season Kanpyo together with such other ingredients as Shiitoke, Koyadofu, Abura Age, carrots, Gobo with Kikkoman, Ajinomoto and sugar." My wife has not tried this dish, but has used the gourd strips in vegetable soup.

A few years ago advertisements for "New Guinea Beans" appeared in several newspapers in the United States. From the sketch presented it was impossible to tell what the plant was, but I suspected that it was a gourd, and subsequently I learned that it was. Sometime later I saw in a newspaper a photograph of a Mr. Dave Cooke of California with his "super beans" growing upon a trellis, and there was no doubt that these were gourds. From the accompanying article I learned that Mr. Cooke's seeds came from New Guinea, and that, although the natives in New Guinea were supposed to relish them, he found them absolutely tasteless. His chief concern, however, was that one of the beans might fall from the vine and injure someone. This New Guinea "bean" is similar to the Italian edible gourd, which was introduced into this country some years earlier without making much of an impact, and I predict a similar fate for the New Guinea bean. Its nutritional value is not great, but for that matter neither is that of a squash. Some of the edible gourds that I have seen have a thinner and softer rind than do other gourds; this may well result from intentional selection by man.

Although it has been suggested that seeds of gourds are rare in archaeological deposits because they were eaten by man, there are surprisingly few references to the use of seeds as food in historic times. It is on record that the seeds were boiled and eaten cold as an appetizer among country people in China, and that in Africa they are used as a masticatory, are crushed and grated to produce an edible oily paste, and furnish an oil used in cooking. I have sampled uncooked seeds. It is no easy task to remove the hard seed coat, but I found the kernel to have a pleasant nutlike taste. The seeds are reported to contain saponins, however; if large amounts were present, one would expect the seed to have a bitter taste, and perhaps be toxic as well, if eaten in large quantities. It is surprising that the seeds, unless they do contain large amounts of saponins, have been so largely ignored as food, for they contain both appreciable amounts of oil and 5 per cent protein. The subject invites further inquiry. Leaves of the gourd have also been used as food in China and some other places.

Medicine and Surgery

Although the medicinal uses of the bottle gourd are fewer than of some of the other kinds of gourds previously treated,

Cutting gourd strips for food in Japan. From the *Sketch Books* of Katsushika Hokusai (1849).

Hanging gourd strips to dry in Japan. From the *Sketch Books* of Katsushika Hokusai (1849).

the number is still impressive. The greatest use in medicine appears to have been in India. The seeds were taken internally for headaches, the oil of the seeds was applied externally for the same purpose, and an infusion of the steeped seeds was drunk for curing chills. The pulp of the gourd has been used as a purgative, apparently more commonly for horses than for humans. The pulp was also considered useful against coughs, as an antidote for certain poisons, and, when applied externally, as a cooling application to the shaved head of a person in delirium. The leaves, which are also purgative, were taken in decoction for jaundice, and the juice of the leaves has been used to cure baldness.* The neck of a gourd was eaten for colic and the head of the person bathed in the water in which the gourd was boiled. The juice of the immature gourd was added to lime juice for treating pimples. Although I have used the past tense to describe these uses, probably many of them still persist in various places.

The surgical operation of trepanation or trephination, involving the removal of a piece of the skull, was practiced in pre-Columbian Peru. It is thought that the operation was performed to repair injuries to the skull, which was often broken by war clubs, and it is reported to have been practiced by Andean Indians even in the early part of this century. To replace the portion of the skull that was removed, a piece of gourd was sometimes inserted and the skin stitched back together over it. In some cases the skull was repaired with thin plates of gold.

Reports of the use of the narrow end of the gourd for giving enemas have come from both Ghana and Hawaii.

Floats and Rafts

The use of gourds as fish-net floats has been previously mentioned, and such use is still fairly widespread. They were

---

*Several of my friends have asked me why I haven't tried it.

also used in fishing in other ways—as fish-line supports in the southeastern United States and to make artificial lures and fish-line reels in Hawaii.

Gourds have also been used as floats for swimmers, somewhat in the fashion of the old water wings. Two gourds were tied together with a string or rope, which was placed under the arms, and the gourds would serve to support a person in the water. Korean women divers used gourds as supports between dives.

From the use of gourds as floats, the idea would easily arise of supporting a raft with gourds, holding them together in a net or attached under a wooden platform. Such rafts are known from India, Africa, Mexico, and South America. In Mexico up to a hundred gourds were used to make a raft. Some of the rafts used for fishing had a platform on which the boatman stood and from which he propelled the raft by means of a stick. In Lake Chad and the Cameroons some of the gourds had hinged lids so that they could also serve as a receptacle for fish. All of the records that I have seen of gourd rafts come from rivers and lakes, and insofar as I am aware no one has suggested that man ever crossed the ocean on a gourd raft. Whether or not it is possible I shall let Thor Heyerdahl determine.

Another rather unusual use of a gourd as a float deserves inclusion, particularly in view of the shark scare that has recently swept over this country. In past times Hawaiian fishermen carried gourds in their canoes, and when a shark was sighted a gourd was thrown overboard with a loud splash to attract its attention. While the shark was occupied in attacking the bobbing gourd, the fishermen had time to head for shore.

Gourd floats also served for the capture of ducks. The Chaco Indians of South America would leave gourds in the water for several days so that the ducks would become used to them, then, concealing themselves among the gourds, they would swim to where the birds were and pull them down by their legs. Such a usage of gourds also is reported from China.

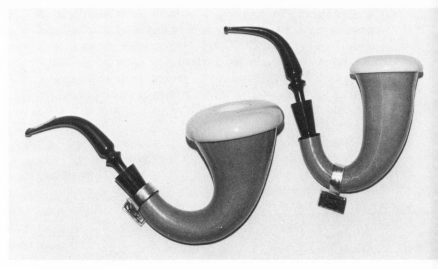

Calabash pipes.

Pipes and Snuffboxes

In parts of Asia and Africa kalians, hookahs, or water pipes were made from gourds, such pipes being used for smoking marijuana or tobacco. A clay bowl was usually inserted in the gourd to hold the hemp or tobacco, the smoke was then drawn through the water in the gourd, and the narrow end of the gourd or a bamboo tube served as the mouthpiece. In Asia the gourds were frequently decorated with silver or brass, and in Africa the gourds were often incised with geometrical patterns or figures of animals or men, or were brass-studded. Various-shaped gourds were used; sometimes these were a foot and a half long and nearly as wide.

The calabash pipe, which I first saw in use by Basil Rathbone in his portrayal of Sherlock Holmes in the movies, is

Gourd snuffbox from bazaar in Samarkand, 1977 (actual size, 5.5 cm.). (Courtesy of Dieter Wilken.)

still widely used. These pipes originally came from South Africa, where special types of gourds with straight necks were artificially altered during growth to produce the desired shape. Only the neck end of the gourd is used for the pipe; a bowl of clay, porcelain, or meerschaum is placed in the large end of the neck; and a bit, or stem, of any one of various materials is affixed to the smaller end. According to some smokers with whom I have discussed the subject, the calabash is superior to a briar pipe. Calabash pipes may be purchased from a number of pipe companies in the United States.

In central Asia small gourds were used to make snuffboxes by a rather elaborate process. Two wooden plates, one of which had an engraved pattern or design, were tied to a young growing gourd with thread. At maturity this gourd would have two flat sides, one of which would have taken on the pattern. The pulp and seeds were removed from the gourd, which then was filled with vegetable oil and placed in manure. The oil in combination with the acids in the manure gave a rich brown color to the gourd. A second method used was to remove the epidermis from the gourd and paint it in various colors with lacquers. About 1930, the last date for which I have information, such snuffboxes could be seen for sale on every corner in the "old city" of Samarkand.*

Cricket Gourds

In "early antiquity" the Chinese began keeping crickets in cages because they enjoyed their singing. About 1000 A.D. they began to hold cricket fights, and many songs and stories dealing with crickets may be found in Chinese literature.

---

*A friend of mine, Dieter Wilken, visited Samarkand in 1977 and found gourd boxes still for sale in the bazaar. He reports that the shape of the gourd is no longer modified, but that the designs on the gourd's surface are still prepared in the same way.

Chinese cricket gourds. (From Laufer, 1927; courtesy of Lorin I. Nevling and the Field Museum of Natural History, Chicago.)

Cricket fights became extremely popular, and contests were regularly held in the autumn. The contestants were matched according to size, and champions were decided in lightweight, medium-weight, and heavyweight classes. Bets were made on the outcomes, and it is said that the aggregate bets in a tournament reached $100,000 at one time. The victories were occasions for great celebration. The names of the winners were inscribed, sometimes in gold, on ivory tablets carved in the shape of a gourd and became prized possessions of the owners of the winning crickets. In short, cricket fights became as celebrated as baseball or boxing is in the United States today.

The catching and raising of crickets became something of an art in China. The gourd enters the story because it served as the winter home of pet crickets. The gourd used was a rather small one; it is said to have been a specially cultivated variety, the cultivation of which was once known to but a single family of Peking. From the examples that I have seen, however, they appear to be rather similar to some of the small gourds that have a very wide distribution today. What is special about the cricket gourds is that they were often decorated with figures or scenes in high relief. A technique that is now lost was used to produce the decorations. Earthen molds with figures in intaglio were placed around the young ovary, and as this grew into a fruit it took on the design from the mold. Wooden structures used to make the clay molds are in the collection of the Peabody Museum of Salem, Massachusetts. The molds, of course, had to be broken to remove the gourds, so new ones had to be made every time a decorated cricket gourd was desired.

The most recent information I have on cricket raising in China is from 1927. Chinese friends tell me they doubt that cricket raising has survived under the Communist regime, as idleness and pleasure are now frowned upon.

Birdhouses

Gourds can be seen as birdhouses in various parts of the United States today. Although it is not known for certain, it is thought that Indians in the southeastern United States may have originated this usage. The gourd birdhouses apparently were used to induce martins to nest near planted fields. The Indians were doubtlessly aware that these birds consumed insects, as well as driving away crows and blackbirds

Birdhouses made from gourds.

at planting time. Birdhouses were still found among these Indians at the time Speck wrote his book on gourds in 1940. A long-necked gourd was given an opening midway to fit the body of the martin and a few drainage holes in the bottom. Sometimes one may get unwanted visitors to his birdhouse. This year I found that yellow jackets had moved into a gourd birdhouse in my backyard. Bees may also use gourds for building a hive.

Hawaiian boatmen with gourd masks. From Captain James Cook and Captain James King, *A Voyage to the Pacific Ocean* (London, 1785).

Masks

Records of gourds being used for masks are known from the United States, Hawaii, and New Zealand. The Catawbas and Cherokees of the southeastern United States made such masks; their use has persisted until fairly recently in the Booger Dance of the Cherokees. These masks had holes for the eyes and mouth and an elongate nose formed by the neck of the gourd. The nose also served as a phallic symbol. Gourd masks were also used by the Hopis of Arizona in certain of their ceremonial dances. Gourd masks or helmets

Hawaiian with gourd mask. From Captain James Cook and Captain James King, *A Voyage to the Pacific Ocean* (London, 1785).

141

from Hawaii are shown in the plates of Captain Cook's account of his third voyage to the Pacific. The exact purpose of these masks is not known, but it is supposed that they were worn for some ceremonial occasion. From New Zealand there is an account of a handsome chief who, when traveling, wore a gourd mask to protect his face from the sun and also to prevent the various women he met from falling in love with him because of his beauty.

Games

In Hawaii a game called *kilu* utilized the top of a gourd, also called *kilu*. A player tried to spin his *kilu* to hit that of his opponent. The game must have been taken quite seriously, for Dodge has written, "If anyone disturbed the silence that was supposed to prevail during the course of the game his clothing was set on fire."

Charms and Offerings

Skeat in his *Malay Magic* (London, Macmillan, 1900) writes that in an elephant hunt it was necessary for the hunter to mask his odor and that of his gun. For this purpose leaves of the bottle gourd, along with certain other leaves, were used. The midrib of the leaf was broken with the left hand and with the eyes closed the hunter said, "As these leaves smell, so may my body be scented."

Professor Friedrich Bischoff of Indiana University's East Asian Department informs me that the gourd has sexual connotations in China. Shou Hsing, the god of longevity, is often portrayed holding a stick on which hangs a scroll and a gourd. The scroll is said to contain the recipe for preserving one's vital power (sexual potency) and the gourd to contain the elixir of life (sperm).

Organ in his book on gourds states that gourds three feet in length were placed in the temples in India as an offering by women whose breasts were poorly developed.

Other Uses

In Angola two small gourds connected by a string have served as telephones in much the same fashion as tin cans have been used by children in the United States. I would assume that this is a very recent use, but I have no information to support my belief.

In Tennessee a long-handled gourd known, for reasons that I do not know, as the Punger gourd, was used as a back scratcher. According to an item in *The Gourd Seed*, laws were passed that prohibited the taxation of this possession.

Other minor uses of the gourd might be listed, but it is time to turn to an important usage, as an article of clothing, for which a whole chapter is needed.

New Guinean with elongate penis sheath.

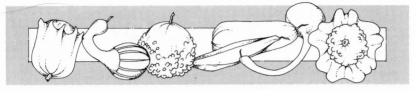

12.
Uses:
Penis Sheaths

As articles of clothing, gourds have been used as hats in the Philippines and in Africa and as a covering for the penis in various parts of the world. The latter is often an indispensable item of attire, not infrequently the only one, and it is the gourd penis sheath, or phallocrypt, if the reader prefers that word, that will be the principal subject of this chapter. For everyday wear man has used many objects to cover the penis—bamboo tubes, horns, coconuts, ivory, wood, shells, leather, grass or other leaves, nets, and cocoons; more recently, toothpaste containers, Kodak film cans, and even sardine tins have been observed used for this purpose in New Guinea.

Why man should wear a penis sheath has been the subject of speculation by both anthropologists and behaviorists. It has been suggested that it may have been for protection, but this is hard to accept when so much else of the body is left exposed. Moreover, in the same region some tribes may wear penis sheaths and others do without them entirely. Why, it also may be asked, would a gourd two feet long be needed when a much smaller one would give quite adequate protection? Some have suggested that it is a shame covering, and

New Guinean with small penis sheath. (Courtesy of Betsy H. Gagné.)

Jalé warriors of western New Guinea. (Courtesy of Klaus-Friedrich Koch.)

today some of the people who wear penis sheaths say it is for modesty's sake and they would not think of appearing in public without one. In fact, when one anthropologist tried to buy a gourd sheath from a man in New Guinea, the man carefully turned his back and affixed another gourd before selling the one he had been wearing. Here again it might be asked, if it is indeed a shame covering, why a gourd two feet long? Others have suggested that it is obviously a display symbol to emphasize virility. If it is a display object, it is not clear whether it is directed toward females or other males,

147

Major geographical areas of penis sheathing. Penis gourds are known from areas shown in black; other types of penis sheaths used in stippled areas; archaeological evidence of penis sheathing in cross-hatched area. (Redrawn from Ucko, 1970.)

148

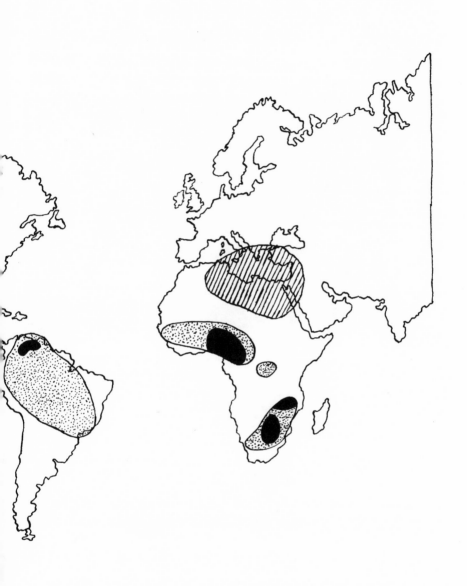

Penis gourds from Dugum Danis of West Irian growing in Indiana.

or both. It is of interest to note that some people who have adopted trousers still insist on wearing an exposed penis sheath, no easy task. The comparison of the penis sheath has been made with the codpieces worn in Europe from the fourteenth to seventeenth century, but investigators have been unable to learn of any sexual significance being attached to the gourds; in spite of the fact that one anthropologist has interpreted the penis sheath to represent a super erection, no deep symbolic meaning has yet been clearly demonstrated.*

*Karl G. Heider (*Man*, n.s. XI [1976], 188–201) has found that the Danis of New Guinea, who wear penis sheaths, have an extremely low level of sexual interest and activity.

It is, of course, possible that the original reason, or reasons—for there could have been more than one—for wearing them has long ago disappeared. In any event, the penis sheath remains an ambiguous object, serving both to conceal and yet emphasize the sexuality of the wearer.

Penis sheathing in historical times is known mainly from Africa, northern South America, and the southwest Pacific. I have seen the statement made that the use of penis gourds is confined to New Guinea, and it is here that it appears to have reached its maximum development; but gourd wearers are also known from southeastern and east central Africa, and the early Spanish explorers found the gourds worn in Venezuela, where they were often decorated with gold and pearls. Gourds as penis sheaths have long since disappeared in South America. The Spanish rapidly acquired those that were decorated with precious metals and stones.

Although outsiders' knowledge of gourd wearing in New Guinea has only recently been acquired, today we know far more about the trait for that region than for any other, and the remainder of this account will be largely confined to New Guinea.

As might be expected, some nonsense has been written about the penis gourd. For example, in the book *Journey into the Stone Age* by David M. Davies (1969), we find that in some unnamed valley in New Guinea the penis gourd is a status symbol, and the men wear gourds that are a yard or more in length. It is supposedly the women of the tribe who select the gourd and fit it on the penis. "The wives of the men who have the biggest gourds" when at a social gathering with their men "swell with pride . . . as they measure up their husband's [gourd] against the lesser fry." The truth in regard to the penis gourd hardly needs such embroidery.

A number of different sizes and shapes of gourds are used in New Guinea. Usually there is a more or less standard type for a given group of people; in general, small globular gourds are found in the northern part and elongate ones, in the central highlands. The latter, sometimes reaching lengths of sixty centimeters, or about two feet, may be quite slender, straight or curved at the tip, and are commonly worn erect; others are rather broad—one writer compares them to a blunderbuss—and may be worn erect or at a forty-five-degree angle. At the other extreme are the gourds that are only slightly larger than an egg and cover only the tip of the penis, which is carried in the normally dangling fashion. Pear-shaped gourds are also used, and in some places two gourds are used, one being inserted into the other to get the desired size.

Some of the people who wear the small gourds have larger globular ones which are worn only during fertility dances that are held to stimulate the growth of crop plants. Among the Umedas the dance gourds are worn with belts which have hard seeds mounted on them, and as the gourd flies upward during the dance it strikes the seeds, giving a clinking sound in time to the music from an orchestra of trumpets. Another group of the Umedas are reported to place small pebbles in the gourds so that they also serve as rattles during the dance.

Among some people the gourds are unadorned, although they may be treated with heat to assume a yellow color and then rubbed with pig's fat or other substances to increase the shine. Other groups engrave the gourds, particularly the globular kinds, with geometrical designs or figures of animals. In the movie "The Gourd Men of New Guinea" it is stated that among the Umedas these designs indicate the ancestral background of the individual wearing it. Although I can think of no more appropriate place to carry such information, I am not sure that this statement is correct, for Jell, who worked among the same people, states that his informants attached no significance to the decorations, although they varied from individual to individual.

The tips of the gourds are sometimes cut off and the hole stuffed with various substances. Among some people the gourds have a tuft of animal fur placed in or at the tip, and the same person who postulated that the gourd symbolized an erection has interpreted this to represent the ejaculate.

Umeda cassoway dancer. (Redrawn from Gell, 1971.)

Sometimes a tassel of fur or a moth's cocoon is placed near the tip, and colored seeds also may be used for decorating the gourd.

In the area where gourds are used as penis sheaths, they are apparently worn at nearly all times by older boys, who often may have a rather small gourd, and adults, who wear larger ones. In some places the old men wear smaller gourds than the younger ones. At times even the male babies may be seen with a token gourd attached to their waist string. In one area, only simple-minded men go around without gourds. Among some people the gourd is worn even while sleeping, and there is one report that urination is performed without removal of the gourd. Some people, however, are known to remove their gourds when engaged in muddy field work. Among the Dugum Danis the men have a complete wardrobe of gourds, some straight, some curved, but it couldn't be determined if a man selected his gourd according to his mood or for a particular occasion.

The attachment of the gourd varies with the type of gourd used. The small globular ones as well as the larger dance gourds are kept on by friction alone, but the elongate ones must be attached by string. Holes are bored in the gourd, usually two near the base for a string that is tied around the scrotum and two higher up for attaching a string around the waist. The men manage very well even with the largest gourds, as, for example, in a battle chase, but sometimes the gourds do come off when they are going through the brush, or become broken, or sometimes in a dance the men may collide and their gourds become entangled. Broken gourds are sometimes repaired by sewing or by inserting the tip of another gourd into the broken one. Among the Kapauku Papuans, the only group for which such information is available, the gourds have a life expectancy of about six months.

Although the penis gourd usually serves solely as a covering for the penis, some of the wearers are reported to use the gourds as repositories for small objects, and others have used them as holders for smoking cigars. They have not been

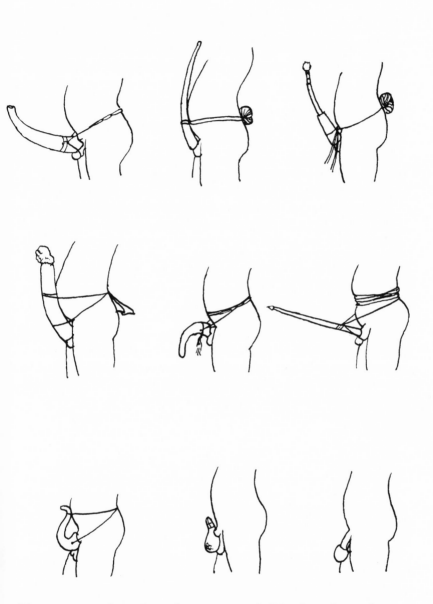

Various ways of attaching the penis gourd. (Mostly redrawn from LeRoux, 1948.)

used as musical instruments, so far as is known, in New Guinea, although some people have attempted to play upon museum specimens of penis sheaths in Europe under the mistaken impression that they were some kind of trumpet.

In considering the origin of the penis sheath, we are confronted with a problem previously discussed. Did this trait arise only once and then diffuse to other parts of the world or did it originate in several different places? Both views have had their proponents. A geographer, M. D. W. Jeffreys, has no hesitation in claiming that the penis sheath and Basenji dog were carried to both the Caribbean and New Guinea on pre-Columbian Arabian voyages. An anthropologist, Peter J. Ucko, who has made a careful study of penis confinement, concludes that only a limited range of solutions exists for covering the penis, that some of these are very simple, and that the simpler the device the more likely it is to have been independently invented.

The concern here is not with penis sheaths in general, for whether or not penis sheathing is a single trait or of multiple origins is beyond the scope of this inquiry. It is not known if gourds were man's first penis sheaths, but we may inquire as to whether the use of gourds as a penis sheath was the result of diffusion or independent invention.

One might postulate that a boatload of people arrived in America from Africa in early times and that the men wore penis gourds. It is unlikely that the penis gourds would have had seeds in them, so one might also postulate that these people brought gourds with seeds in them. However, this is unnecessary if, as has already been suggested, gourds already grew in America when man arrived from Africa. Thus, penis gourd sheathing could have been introduced from Africa to America without the people necessarily bringing seeds with them. It seems fruitless to pursue this argument for the Americas—one could speculate endlessly—but it should be pointed out again that it is far from certain that men from Africa ever reached South America in pre-Columbian times.

The situation in New Guinea, however, does merit more

The Danis preparing a field for growing sweet potatoes. (Courtesy of D. E. Yen and the Bishop Museum Press, Honolulu.)

consideration. A few years ago it occurred to me that it could be worth the effort to learn more about the gourds of New Guinea. Accordingly, I started another letter-writing campaign, and as a result I secured seed samples of six different gourds from three different parts of the island. One of these gourds was used for penis sheaths, three were used for food or containers, and the use of the other two was not specified.

This is a very small sample, and I would have desired more before reaching any conclusions. But, nevertheless, they did provide some information on the gourds of New Guinea. Without going into details, for these have been published elsewhere, I shall summarize the results. In most features these gourd plants were more like those of the African-American race than those of the Asiatic race. The seeds, however, were more similar to those of the Asian gourds.

Had the gourds clearly fallen into the Asiatic race, which is rather what I had expected, there would have been little difficulty in explaining their presence in New Guinea. Or had they been clearly like the African-American gourds, we could have more readily postulated an introduction from Africa or the Americas. But, as it is, we must explain why these gourds have several features of the African-American race but are not identical to any of them. Obviously, all that we can do is speculate.

If gourds floated from Africa to America, as has been suggested, obviously they might have floated to other areas, although floating from either Africa or the Americas to New Guinea would be rather unlikely because of the prevailing direction of the ocean currents. If, however, this did happen, how are we to account for the differences in the seeds of the gourds of New Guinea from those of the African and American ones? Perhaps this could have been a local differentiation or perhaps it could have resulted from hybridization with an Asian type that was already present in New Guinea or that was later introduced. It may well be asked, however, if gourds floated to New Guinea from either Africa or the Americas, why aren't similar types of gourds found in other islands in that part of the world? The answer is that our knowledge of gourds from that area is so limited that we can't say definitely what type, if any, occurred in the other islands.

It is perhaps more reasonable to postulate an introduction of gourds to New Guinea by man. Gourds are known archaeologically from New Guinea at 300 B.C. One might suggest a very early introduction of gourds by man either directly from Africa or South America, perhaps with their use as a penis sheath, but, if so, the problem of explaining the differences in the seeds remains the same as before. It is perhaps easier to accept an early introduction from southeastern Asia along with certain other food plants which are known in New Guinea. To do so, however, an explanation is required to account for the gourds of New Guinea being more similar to those of Africa and the Americas. One might then postulate that the original type of gourd entered Asia from Africa, was carried to New Guinea in an early migration, and persisted in New Guinea with little change, whereas differentiation took place in Asia. The newly differentiated types of gourd *(asiatica)* replaced the original type in Asia and spread to the Pacific region, except for New Guinea. Another possibility is that there was an early introduction of an Asian gourd into New Guinea and that the present New Guinea type differentiated there. The similarities of the New Guinea gourds to the American and Asian ones then might be explained as the result of parallel evolution in a similar type of environment (tropical rain forest?) in these three areas. The seeds, however, retained some features of the Asian subspecies.

It all becomes very complicated, and I have speculated perhaps much more than my small sample of gourds allows. However, I do not see that there is any strong reason to assume that the two events—the introduction of gourds into New Guinea and their adoption as penis sheaths—are necessarily related, although I have certainly not proved that they are not. Moreover, I think that it will be most difficult, if not impossible, to prove that the wearing of penis gourds in widely separated parts of the world is the result of cultural diffusion or independent invention. Certainly, life will go on if we do not know the answer, although man always hates to leave any mystery unsolved. My personal opinion is that it probably required no great flash of genius for man to adopt a gourd for a penis sheath, and I find it difficult to believe that it could not have occurred more than once. From certain rather crude remarks made by some visitors to my garden of gourds, I feel that the association of certain gourds with penes must not be uncommon. Some of the visitors I am sure were totally unaware that gourds have been used as penis sheaths. I have no evidence, however, that any of them subsequently adopted gourds for such use.

Just as this book was going to press, I had a visit from Dr. Barbara Pickersgill, who was returning to England after having spent several months teaching in New Guinea. She reported that penis gourds are now being sold to tourists in various shops, including those operated by the YMCA and the Girl Guides, in Port Moresby.

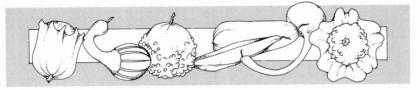

13.
Uses:
Decorated Gourds

Almost everywhere the bare surface of the gourd has been inviting to man for artistic expression. Our earliest record of decorated gourds comes from coastal archaeological sites in Peru dated to 2000 B.C. Although the practice of decorating gourds has disappeared in some places, it lives on in many parts of the world and, in fact, may be more widespread today than ever before. Decorating gourds is a secular activity in most places today, but it could well be that it owes its origin to magico-religious motives. The gourd was most important to primitive people, and thus became incorporated in their religious observances. Today among the Chokwes' of Angola the gourd has magical uses for protection against evil spirits or illness, and it is generally painted and decorated in various ways. Among them it is a fundamental object to be used for charms and amulets and in various magical rites; it is often buried with them. Barbara Rubin has written that among the Fulanis of Nigeria the women seemed to fear that great harm would come to their cattle if they sold her the decorated gourds or told her too much about the meanings of the motifs. Only with great secrecy was she able to buy gourds from one woman, who decided she would report that the gourds had been broken rather than chance a beating from her husband for endangering the cattle by telling him that she had sold them.

Although originally it was the gourds used for bottles, bowls, rattles, and so on that were decorated, in time the decoration became the primary end in itself; today in many places gourds are decorated solely for selling. They have become popular tourist items, particularly in Peru and parts of west Africa. The motifs have sometimes changed over the years, but the techniques, except for employing metal tools, appear to be little changed from the ancient ways. Carving and pyroengraving are methods of decorating gourds in many places in the world; so too is the use of geometrical designs, flowers, animals, and domestic scenes as motifs. One might argue that this implies cultural diffusion, but apparently there are only a limited number of ways of decorating a gourd, and they could all well result from several independent inventions. If, on the other hand, it could be shown that the intricate geometrical patterns on the gourds from various parts of the world show great similarity, a strong case might be made for cultural diffusion. In this connection it should be noted that hieroglyphs that are thought to convey messages are found on gourds from Africa, South America, and Easter Island.

Gourds are usually decorated after they are completely dry. The thin epidermis is usually removed it if has not already weathered off. To accomplish this the gourd is usually soaked in water, after which the outer skin is easily peeled or scraped off. Sometimes whole gourds are used, but more often the gourd is cut in half or the top cut off, depending on the purpose it is to serve, and the seeds and dried pulp are removed and the inside smoothed. The outside of the gourd is then polished with some variety of rough herb. The gourd then may be decorated in this state—its natural yellow-tan color, which is not unattractive—or it may be stained various colors by the use of natural dyes.

The pattern or design is traced on the gourd with a pencil or sharp tool. It is then incised with a knife or chisel, a

A Peruvian decorating a gourd by pyroengraving. (Courtesy of Julia Zagar.)

Decorated gourd from Peru. (Courtesy of Leslie Miller.)

Decorated gourd from Peru. (Courtesy of Eleanor Menzie.)

process sometimes known as pressure engraving, and may be left in this state. Among some gourd carvers the background around the patterns or figures is scraped away so that the figure is raised. Frequently, by means of a hot tool—several of which are usually used so that they can be kept at the correct temperature—the gourd is scorched or burned (pyroengraving). The amount of pressure and time used determines the shade of color that results, so that it is possible to obtain several shades from a light brown or tan to a dark brown or black. Sometimes the engraving itself is done with a hot tool.

165

Stones or silver may be affixed to the gourd for further decoration.

Although gourd decoration was practiced in several parts of the Americas, its occurrence in Peru is most noteworthy. In that country engraved gourds have traditionally come from three regions, Catacaos on the north coast, and near Huancayo and Huanta in the central highlands. Today there are also artisans in Lima to help supply the demands of the tourist trade. Certain people have been widely recognized as artists, but a number of the gourds now being sold appear to be rather hastily made. Most are produced by a combination of cold pressure and pyroengraving techniques. Some are stained, purple and green being the most popular colors. The methods of staining are sometimes trade secrets, as I learned when I asked an artisan in Lima to explain her method. On the north coast, acids reportedly are used—sulphuric for a dark color, hydrochloric for an orange color, and nitric for yellow. Scenes of domestic life, both modern and Indian, and fiestas are often portrayed on the gourds, and llamas are most popular among the animal subjects. With the advantage of their natural shape, some gourds are made to resemble animals, rodents and fish being commonly represented.

Gourd decoration apparently is even more widely practiced in Africa than in the Americas. The studies of Barbara Rubin provide us with a fine description of the techniques used in the northeast state of Nigeria. Throughout this area gourd decoration is women's work. Pyroengraving is the most common technique, although in some parts pressure engraving is employed. The two processes are not combined as in Peru. In some places the old artists are still remembered, and their gourds are preserved as heirlooms. Among the Teras today certain women are admired as artists and their gourds are much sought. In one place, among the Fulanis, a red color is added to the gourd after pyroengraving. A paste of sorghum stalks boiled with cottonseed oil is applied to the area that is to take the color, the other parts having previously been

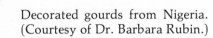

Decorated gourds from Nigeria.
(Courtesy of Dr. Barbara Rubin.)

A Nigerian carving a gourd. (Fosca Photo Services.)

masked with mud. In another place a red color is obtained from a mixture of sorghum stems, indigo, and pods of the tamarind. Pressure engraving is done with thin lines, following which a mixture of peanut oil and soot is rubbed over the gourd. It is then rubbed with dry earth so that a black residue remains only in the engraved lines.

In other parts of Africa men may be the gourd carvers. A particularly celebrated artist, Madya, is known from Zaire. His gourds have been widely exhibited and much sought by Europeans. His principal tool is a pocket knife, which serves both to scratch in the outline and for the actual carving. Two heated irons are used to darken the surface and for shading to give a greater impression of depth. Kaolin is added for whitening to accentuate the relief or to point up some detail. The gourd is finally polished with oil from a palm nut to give a varnishlike finish to the surface.

Still another type of decorated gourd comes from Nigeria. I have not seen these described, and my only knowledge of them comes from a few that I have seen on sale in this country and from photographs sent to me by G. A. Akintola. Apparently they are made in the following manner. The outermost part of the rind of a whole gourd or a section of a large gourd is removed by scraping.* A design is then made on the gourd and the background cut away entirely. The result is an attractive, extremely lightweight piece. The ones that I have seen are not colored, but are left in their natural, almost white, state.

In the Pacific region gourd decoration was well known in both Hawaii and New Zealand. The decoration of gourds was discontinued in Hawaii shortly after the arrival of European culture. Many of the gourds, however, survive in museums. There are several accounts of the methods used, but there is considerable disagreement among them. The most common method appears to have been incision with fine lines, but a few examples are preserved that appear to have been done by pyroengraving. From some accounts of the methods it seems that the gourds were carved while still green. Various herbs were used for staining, and some reports suggest that the stain was applied on the inside of the gourd, which was then placed in an oven for three or four days or buried in mud for a period of time to complete the dying process. The result was a brown or black gourd with the design in white or yellow.

According to Dodge, the decoration of gourds among the Maoris in New Zealand "has long since been abandoned."

---

*I have found that a wood file can be used to scrape away the surface quite readily, but I do not know what kind of a tool is used in Nigeria.

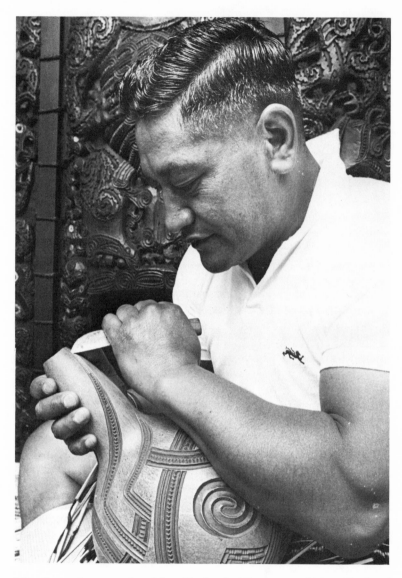

Maori carving gourd in New Zealand. (Courtesy of New Zealand *Herald and Weekly News*, Aukland.)

However, I received a newspaper account from W. R. Sykes in 1970 that indicates the practice still survives. The method used is pressure engraving, and the bold designs are a striking contrast to those of Hawaii.

Matés

No account of decorated gourds would be complete without some discussion of the matés of southern South America. *Maté* is the Quechuan word for "gourd," and was extended to a vessel or cup made from the gourd. The latter is used for drinking a tea brewed from the leaves of a shrub or small tree, *Ilex paraguariensis*. The tea is called "Paraguay tea" or "Jesuits' tea" in English, and *yerba maté* or simply *maté* in Spanish. Thus, we have several meanings of the word *maté*—the gourd, the vessel, the tea, and the plant that gives the tea.

The Guaranis of South America had discovered at some unknown time that the tea brewed from the leaves of *Ilex paraguariensis* made a stimulating beverage. When the Spanish entered South America, they adopted the drink, and the Jesuits brought the plant into cultivation. Today the plant is widely grown in southern South America, and its tea is drunk by millions of people, taking the place of coffee or tea among us. A caffeinelike substance is responsible for its stimulating properties.

The Spanish adopted the Indian's gourd for brewing the tea and devised a straw, or *bombilla*, for drinking it from the maté. The original *bombilla* was a cane straw with a filter of vegetable fibers at the end to prevent the crushed leaves from entering the tube. This was eventually replaced by a metal structure with a mouthpiece, a long tube, and a filter. Today a number of different types of metal *bombillas* are in use, some of them made of silver and elaborately ornamented.

Although simple, unadorned gourds are still frequently used for drinking maté, the matés, too, are often elaborately decorated. One of the earliest steps was to cover the mouth of the gourd with a metal collar, or rim, which prevented the gourd from breaking so readily. Later the base of the gourd was also covered with metal, which further protected it and, by providing a flat base, allowed it to sit on a table more easily. Sometimes a tripod was added for the same reason. Eventually silver and gold leaf were used in various ways so that matés became objects of beauty and in time family heirlooms and museum pieces. From strictly utilitarian objects, matés evolved into objects for admiration, true works of art, some of which I doubt have ever been used for brewing maté.

Several different types of gourds are used, some of which are preferred over others because they are more easily cleaned and handled and less prone to break. In Argentina the gourds used are generally rather small, holding slightly less than a cup of liquid, but in Brazil larger gourds that hold nearly a quart may be used. Gourds for matés, which are grown on a commercial scale in some parts of Argentina, are said to require no cultivation after they are planted.

The tea, of course, may be drunk from any type of cup, but according to the *aficionados* of maté, the drink is not the same when anything other than a gourd is used. As Villanueva says, using anything other than a gourd for a maté is like using a new gourd every time; it gives a drink "without intimacy, without reminiscence, without heart, without poetry, without character." It is the porosity of the gourd that gives it the special properties so that the flavor improves with the aging of the gourd. Maté may be served with sugar or cream and sugar, but confirmed drinkers feel that the only real beverage is maté *amargo*, made directly from the leaves without the addition of any adulterants. It is also Villanueva who reports that jealous wives prefer matés with handles, for then there is no opportunity for a husband to touch hands when accepting maté from the *cebadora* (a woman who brews maté).

George Gaylord Simpson, the well-known biologist, has

Elaborately decorated maté with *bombilla* from Chile. (Courtesy of Museum of Fine Arts, Boston.)

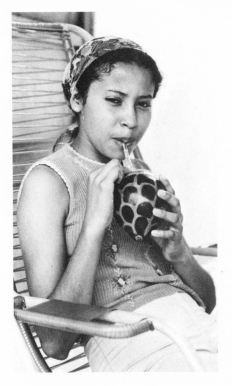

Girl drinking maté in southern Brazil. (Courtesy of James Coleman.)

provided a fascinating account of maté in his *Attending Marvels*. Simpson went to Patagonia in 1930 to collect fossils, and while there he became very fond of maté, which he tells us is the center of social life, if not life in general, in Patagonia. Maté is drunk on every possible occasion, or on no occasion at all, and some people drink as much as twenty to a hundred matés a day, although about twenty a day satisfied him. After discussing the preparation of the tea, he writes about the gourd.

There are other things that must be known in order to make mate amargo properly. For instance, a new gourd must never be used. When one must be purchased, it is filled with damp yerba of good quality and allowed to stand for several days, renewing the water from time to time and taking care that it does not ferment. The inside of the gourd is lightly porous, and it soaks up the essence and becomes seasoned, like an old pipe. This makes a surprising difference in flavor, apparent even to an untrained taste. The older the gourd is, the better, unless through carelessness it is allowed to ferment or to mould, which spoils it forever. The natives are so reluctant to throw away old seasoned gourds that they will go to almost any lengths to repair cracks or breaks. The way to repair a crack is to take part of a sheep's intestine that is shaped like a little bag, turn it inside out, and put the gourd inside while the intestine is still wet. This shrinks on drying, grasping and compressing the gourd, and becomes hard and leathery. It has, furthermore, an attractive honeycomblike pattern.

In other parts of Argentina broken matés may be repaired by sewing. The gourd is soaked and a horsehair is used for thread.

Simpson goes on to describe how at any gathering, no matter the time of day, maté is served.

The company forms a circle, with the cebador next to the fire. He prepares the yerba, brews and spits out the first gourdful, and then brews the second — and, by the way, no time should be allowed for brewing; it should be drunk immediately after pouring water or it will become too bitter and eventually will turn black. The second mate is passed to the man on the left of the cebador, who drinks it and passes back the gourd, and so on around the circle in rotation. Only one gourd and one bombilla are used, no matter how large the company. This is neither sanitary nor enticing, but one becomes accustomed to anything and either to refuse mate or to insist on a separate bombilla would be insulting.

Gourdcraft

Although the decoration of gourds has disappeared in Hawaii and perhaps other places, it seems in no danger of dying out. In fact, the cultivation and decoration of gourds have become

175

Some of Leslie Miller's decorated gourds.

a growing hobby of many people in the United States. Gourds are pressure engraved, pyroengraved, or painted, and although the ones that I have seen do not achieve the beauty of some of those previously discussed, it is possible that in time true artists will emerge. Among some of the best that I have seen made in this country are those done by Leslie Miller, a mathematics professor at Ohio State University. He uses wood chisels for carving geometrical patterns on the gourd and then applies a walnut stain, wiping off the excess so that carved portions assume a dark color and the remainder of the gourd retains its natural color.

Gourdcraft on exhibit at the Ohio Gourd Show, 1975. The objects shown here were made from various gourds, mostly bottle gourds and loofahs.

Many people also find enjoyment in making use of gourds in other decorative ways. A large variety of animals can be created, taking advantage of the natural shape of gourds and applying a little paint and imagination. Elephants, birds, fish, snakes, and prehistoric animals are favorite subjects. Other decorative and sometimes useful items made from gourds are flowers, lamps, Christmas tree ornaments, wreaths, dolls, hats, and all types of dishes. There is an American Gourd Society with over five hundred members, which publishes a leaflet three times a year to encourage the growing of gourds and their uses in the decorative arts. In some places

177

there are local clubs. One of these, the Ohio Gourd Society, has an annual show in which prizes are awarded for the best gourd displays, the largest gourd, the longest gourd, and winners in various other categories. Gourds are probably more widely grown in the United States today than they were at any time by the Indians.

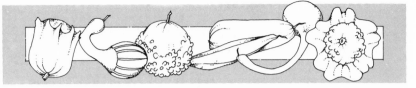

14.
Uses:
Musical Instruments

The use of the gourd for musical instruments was almost as widespread as its use for utensils. Although we may not find gourd instruments in our modern symphonic orchestras, they are still widely used, particularly in folk music, in many parts of the world. Probably only the bamboo rivals the gourd in use for primitive musical instruments. It came as a surprise to me to find that no one has ever done a monograph on gourds as musical instruments; if it has been done, it has escaped my attention. The present treatment is no monograph, but it will provide some idea as to the range of instruments for which gourds are used.

At the risk of becoming monotonous, I should point out that the origin of musical instruments poses the same problem that we have previously encountered. Did each type of instrument have but a single origin, or were there multiple origins? Some people, including Curt Sachs, an authority on musical instruments, believe in a single origin followed by diffusion. For some instruments—the xylophone, for example—a single origin appears most likely; but for others, particularly the rattle, it is not difficult to envisage independent invention in many parts of the world, unless the rattle goes back to some

Gourd rattles from the American Southwest. (Indiana University Museum.)

of the earliest populations of humans, which, of course, may not be out of the question.

Idiophones

The majority of the gourd instruments are "self-sounding," or idiophones, and rattles are most prominent among these. If not man's first musical instruments, rattles were certainly among his earliest ones. Of course, they were also made from a number of materials other than gourds—bark, wood, raw-hide, turtle shells, sea shells, animal bones, even human skulls

Beaded rattle and one-string gourd instrument. (Courtesy of Ghana Information Services.)

—but perhaps there is no more natural rattle than the gourd. Some of them come provided with a neck that may serve as a handle and seeds that, when dry, will produce a sound as the gourd is shaken. Later, it was found that if pebbles were substituted for the seeds a louder sound would result and that wooden handles could be inserted onto gourds without necks. It is not surprising to find, therefore, that gourds were used as rattles almost everywhere they could be grown.

The rattle was more than musical instrument; in the hands of the shaman—medicine man, or witch doctor—it was the source of magic, a means of contacting the spirits and of

Dancers with gourd rattles in Virginia. From drawing by John White in Theodore de Bry's *A Brief and True Report of the New Found Land of Virginia* (1590).

exorcism. It was used in the most important ceremonies of the tribe, from the initiation of youths to burial rites, as well as for curing the ailing and for attaining success in love affairs. In many cultures only the shaman could touch the rattle, whereas in a few only women were permitted to use it. Rattles, of course, were widely used in dances, which

Uli uli rattles from Hawaii.

themselves were often magico-religious rites. They were also used as signaling devices, for transmitting messages, for scaring birds away from the garden, and for marking the movements of domesticated animals. From its rather noble beginnings the rattle has come down to modern cultures chiefly as a toy for babies, and these are now usually made of plastic.

Rattles were often elaborately decorated, which further increased their magical properties. The gourd itself was sometimes carved or pyroengraved, and feathers, beads, or other objects were attached to the handle. In Africa sometimes the gourd is covered by a loose net which is ornamented with shells, bones, metal, or beads, and it is these striking on the gourd that produces the sound. Among the most beautiful rattles are the *uli ulis* of Hawaii, which came to be used in the hula dances. The rattle was made from a highly polished gourd or coconut shell with a short handle inserted into it. The handle was decorated with a circle of red feathers, within

183

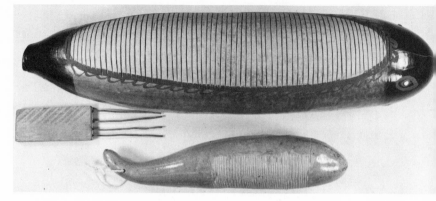

Güiros, or scrapers, from Latin America.

which a smaller circle of gold feathers was placed. Some years ago a disease wiped out the gourd in Hawaii, and today tree gourds, imported from Mexico, are sometimes used to make the *uli ulis.*

Not everyone appreciated the music of the gourd rattle, as is evident from Capt. John Smith's account of the Indians of Virginia.* "Their chief instruments," he writes, "are rattles made of small gourds or pumpeons shells. Of these they have base, tenor, counter-tenor, mean, and treble. These mingled with their voices, sometimes twenty or thirty together, make such a terrible noise as would rather affright than delight any man."

Sometimes more than a single gourd is used to make a rattle, or pieces of gourd may be threaded on a stick to make a

---

*John Smith, *General History of Virginia,* in John Rinkerton's *A General Collection of the Best and Most Interesting Voyages and Travels in all Parts of the World . . .*, Vol. 13 (London, Longman, 1808–14).

"Thumb piano," or *kasai*, Zaire. (Courtesy of Barbara W. Merriam.)

rattling instrument. Although gourds are usually shaken, sometimes they are attached to a stick that is stamped on the ground or hit against the thighs.

Friction idiophones, or scrapers, are instruments in which the sound is created by rubbing a gourd against a board, or a wire or stick against a gourd. So far I have seen accounts of this instrument only from Africa and tropical America, although it may have a more extensive distribution. In the latter region, where it is usually known as a *güiro* (from an Indian word from the West Indies meaning "gourd"), it is usually a small elongate gourd—eight inches to a foot and a half in length—on which a series of closely spaced grooves are made on the surface. Scraping the corrugated surface with a stick or wire brush produces a rather harsh sound that finds a place in Latin rumba music. I have no knowledge of this instrument's place of origin or antiquity.

The *sansa*, *mbirba*, *kasai*, or *deze*, names commonly used in Africa, or the "thumb piano," or "Kaffir piano," as it is frequently incorrectly called in English, is another type of idiophone in which a small soundboard of a tuned series of metal or bamboo strips is placed over or in a resonator. Most frequently a half or three-quarters of a gourd serves as the resonator. The instrument is African, but is sometimes seen in gift stores as well as in museums in the United States.

A xylophone with resonators is frequently called a *marimba*. This instrument has been the subject of considerable investigation. It appears to have originated in Indonesia, where resonators of bamboo were used. It reached Africa quite early, perhaps in the first century following Christ and almost certainly before the Portuguese began their extensive ocean voyages. In Africa gourds became commonly used for resonators. A fine description of one of these instruments is given by G. M. Theal in his *Records of South Eastern Africa* (1901).

The best and most musical of their instruments is called the *ambira*, which greatly resembles our organs; it is composed of long gourds, some very wide and some very narrow, held close together and arranged in order. The narrowest, which form the treble, are placed on the left, contrary to that of our organs, and after the treble come the other gourds with their different sounds of contralto, tenor, and bass, being eighteen gourds in all. Each gourd has a small opening at the side near the end, and at the bottom a small hole the size of a dollar, covered with a certain kind of spider's web, very fine, closely woven, and strong, which does not break. Upon all the mouths of these gourds, which are of the same size and placed in a row, keys of thin wood are suspended by cords so that each key is held in the air above the hollow of its gourd, not reaching the edges of the mouth. The instrument being thus

Gourd xylophone, or marimba. (Courtesy of Ghana Information Services.)

constructed, the Kaffirs play upon the keys with sticks after the fashion of drum-sticks, at the points of which are buttons made of sinews rolled into a light ball of the size of a nut, so that striking the notes with these two sticks, the blows resound in the mouths of the gourds, producing a sweet and rhythmical harmony, which can be heard as far as the sound of a good harpsichord. There are many of these instruments, and many musicians who play upon them very well.

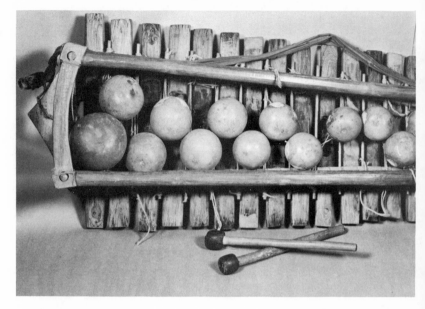

Marimba from Sierra Leone with globular gourds. This instrument is carried when played. (Indiana University Museum.)

In the New World the gourd marimba has become most prominent in Guatemala, where it is widely played by Indians. There is no evidence, however, that it is pre-Columbian in the Americas. The instrument or the idea for the instrument and the name *marimba* (*malimba* in Bantu) came to the New World with slaves. Gourds were, of course, readily available in Guatemala, where they became used as resonators, although sometimes the resonators are made of wood today.

Membranophones

Gourds have been used as drums in several parts of the world. Two gourds mounted together were dropped and slapped for

Close-up of Ghanaian marimba showing the spider's nest buzzers. (Indiana University Museum.)

"music" in Hawaii. Indians in the southwestern United States inverted a half gourd over water; when played, it gave a sound much like that of a drum. The foregoing instruments should be classed as idiophones and not true drums, or membranophones, for they do not employ a membrane stretched over the opening. Such true drums have been found in Africa, however. Gourd drums have also been reported in northern South America, but the source does not state whether or not a membrane was used.

Aerophones

The earliest wind instruments may have been used more for signaling than for producing music. Although it is possible

189

Gourd drums. (Courtesy of Ghana Information Services.)

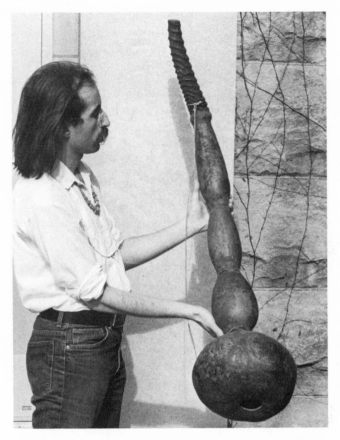

Peter Gold of the Indiana University Museum holding
an African horn made from parts of four gourds with
an antelope horn mouthpiece.

that the first one was made of a gourd, it is just as likely that it was made from an animal's horn, shell, or bamboo. The slender end of a gourd can serve as a flute. By adding holes, various kinds of whistles or ocarinalike instruments can be made; these are common in both South America and Hawaii. In Hawaii whistles served as signaling devices for lovers in the night. The gourd whistles made in China were sometimes attached to pigeons' tails, the sound produced in flight serving to protect them from birds of prey. Although flutes or whistles are usually played with the mouth, among some people the nose is used. The nose whistles from the Matto Grosso of Brazil are made of two small pieces of gourd, mounted together with wax or gum, with three holes. Tops made of gourds are known from Hawaii, the Americas, and Africa. Some of these had a hole in the gourd which when spun produced a whistling or humming sound. They are perhaps better classified as toys than as musical instruments.

Trumpets made of a single piece of gourd or of several pieces joined together were known to the Incas and more recently have been found among the forest tribes of South America and in Africa, Indonesia, and Hawaii. A clarinetlike instrument is also known in which a gourd served as the bell. In India an ancient wind instrument called the *magudi* (also *pungi* or *been* in the northern part of the country) is used by snake charmers and jugglers. The instrument consists of a gourd with two reeds attached. The one description that I have seen states that one reed has four or five finger holes and the other reed, one; however, the one from India in my possession has seven holes in one reed and none in the other, and the two from Pakistan (see photograph) have eight holes in one reed and two in the other.

Cordophones

As a part of a musical instrument, gourds seem to have found their greatest use in string instruments; today, particularly in Africa and India, a large number of such instruments is

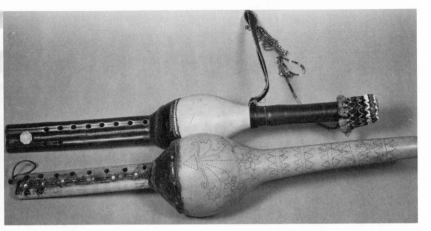

Snake charmers' horns from Pakistan. (Indiana University Museum.)

known with one or more gourds serving as resonators. The gourds used vary in size from some of the smallest to extremely large ones.

The musical bow is thought to be the most primitive string instrument, and its use was very widespread. According to Curt Sachs, the musical bow was one of the first instruments "used for intimacy and to induce meditation. It was considered an effective treatment for communication with the spirits." According to several sources, the musical bow was derived from the hunter's bow, for the hunter would have noted the twang when an arrow was shot. But such an origin is not accepted by all authorities, including Sachs, who points out that in some cultures the musical bow is not associated with hunters and, further, that in many tribes only the women play. Such facts, however, do not necessarily rule out that it was originally derived from the hunting bow. The !Kung of Nyae Nyae today use their hunting bows for musical instruments. According to a legend from East Africa, its ori-

Musical bows in Rwanda.
(Courtesy of Barbara W.
Merriam.)

gin is quite clear. A man is journeying with a woman, and when she bends over to take a drink of water, he breaks her neck. (Why? The reason is not given; the reader will have to supply his own.) The woman is transformed into a musical bow, her head becoming the gourd resonator.

Musical bows are also found in the Americas, where gourd resonators were also used. There has been some question as to whether the instrument was pre-Columbian, some persons feeling that it was introduced to the Americas from

A gourd lute. (Courtesy of Ghana Information Services.)

Africa with the slave trade. The musical bow of western Mexico, as among the Coras, however, is quite a different instrument from that of other parts of America and is played in a different manner. Moreover, it is used in religious ceremonies, whereas in other parts of America the musical bow is used more as a toy. This western Mexican instrument could well be pre-Columbian and, indeed, if it is not an indigenous development, could have come from southeastern Asia rather than Africa.

A string instrument, or *nzenze*, from Zaire.
(Courtesy of Barbara W. Merriam.)

A *kalandin*, a one-string gourd instrument from Guinea. (Courtesy of UNESCO.)

From the musical bow there arose a large number of other string instruments, many of which employ gourds as resonators. In Africa a wide variety of such instruments is found: (1) zithers, including the *mvet* of the Cameroons, which has a gourd resonator in the middle and sometimes smaller ones at either end, and the *sese*, a bar zither; (2) lutes, sometimes covered with the skin of a water lizard, ranging from one-string fiddles, which are quite widespread, to plucked lutes with two to five strings, to twenty-one-string instruments which may have a huge gourd for the resonator; (3) lyres, in some places called *kissars*, one of which now in the Metropolitan Museum of Art has a half-gourd body decorated with geometric designs with a membrane stretched over the open part, two uprights of curved animal horns to which a cross-bar is attached, and eight strings strung from the body to the crossbar.

Instruments similar to some of the African ones are found in southeastern Asia. For example, a bar zither using a gourd or a coconut shell as the resonator is found in the Celebes, but it was in India that the string instruments using gourds were to become most highly developed and appreciated. The simplest of the Indian instruments is the *ektara*, a single-string instrument with a gourd resonator. This is thought to be the precursor of the vina (also veena). There are four basic types of these instruments: the *tambura*, with four strings and a single gourd; the bin, or northern vina, which has gourds of equal size at either end, four playing strings, and three side strings; the vina proper, which is a seven-string instrument with a large wooden body and a gourd near the other end; and the sitar, which may have a wooden or gourd body, usually a smaller gourd at the upper end, and sometimes a small gourd near the body. The sitar, which is now well known in the United States through the music of Ravi Shankar and the Beatles, appeared in the thirteenth century in India. Originally it had three strings, but now it has seven main strings and eleven or twelve sympathetic strings. It is the most common of the stringed instruments in India.

A woman playing the vina. Drawn from a statue in the 1,000-pillared mantapam, India.

The most beloved of these instruments, according to some sources, is the bin. Legend has it that it was created by the Hindu god Shiva, who was inspired by the sight of a lovely girl, whose beautiful breasts rising and falling rhythmically and arms adorned with bracelets to him symbolized music. So intoxicated was he with this sight that he could not rest until he embodied this graceful figure into a musical instrument. The bin was the result, its long neck representing the girl's slender body; the two gourds, her well-formed breasts; the metal frets, her bracelets; and the sound, her breathing.

By some the banjo is thought to be of recent origin and is credited to the United States; but Thomas Jefferson in his *Notes on Virginia,* writing on the musical ability of the blacks, states, "The instrument proper to them is the Banjar which they brought hither from Africa, and which is the original of the guitar, its chords being precisely the four lower chords of the guitar." Whether the origin of the banjo should be credited to the United States I shall let others determine, but certainly its antecedents are African. Slaves made the instruments in the United States and based them upon some of the African instruments, such as the *cora,* which utilized a membrane-covered gourd. The gourds that the blacks found readily available in their new country were also sometimes used to make guitars. Violins or fiddles were also made of gourds, particularly in the Appalachians. Such instruments can sometimes still be seen in use at folk-music festivals.

A woman playing the sitar at Lagore University, India. (Courtesy of UNESCO/Marc Reboud.)

15.
The Gourd in Myth,
Legend, and Fable

Ernest S. Dodge, in his *Gourd Growers of the South Seas*, described as follows the role that gourds played in Polynesia before the arrival of the Europeans in the nineteenth century:

A Polynesian in the pre-European days was probably more conscious of the gourd plant than any other human being on earth. The conditioning of a Hawaiian was particularly influenced by the presence of gourds, and countless were the manifestations of this plant. He was brought up with the myth that the heavens were the top of an enormous gourd, that the earth was its lower half. . . .

One might disagree with Dodge when he says that the Polynesians were probably more conscious of the gourd than any other people, for it was equally important to the inhabitants of many other areas, and we find it has entered the folklore of a great many people. Nowhere is man's appreciation of the gourd better shown than in his incorporation of it not only into the stories of his origin but into those of everyday life as well.

Some years ago one of my daughters, knowing of my interest in gourds, called my attention to a delightful little story from Africa which related that babies came from gourds. Try as I might, I have not been able to relocate this story, but during my search I have turned up a number of other stories about gourds. I can't say that my search was systematic, nor am I qualified to make judgments in the field of folklore, but I do feel that some of the stories deserve inclusion in this book. The gourd, or calabash, as it is frequently called, figures incidentally in many stories, in some it is an essential character, and in others it plays the main role. It is, of course, impossible to be sure which gourd is meant at times, but there can be little doubt that in most cases it is the bottle gourd.

The great significance of the gourd to many people is perhaps no better shown than by its prominence in their creation myths. Thus, from Hawaii we have the following story, the one no doubt to which Dodge made reference.

There is a Hawaiian legend . . . which ascribes the creation of the world to *Wakea* [Vast-expanse] and *Papa* [Rock] in this way: "*Papa*, the wife of *Wakea* begat a calabash—*ipu*—including bowl and cover. *Wakea* threw the cover upward and it became the heaven. From the inside meat and seeds, *Wakea* made the sun, moon, stars and sky, from the juice he made the rain, and from the bowl he made the land and the sea." [1]*

Another myth from Hawaii tells of a young ruler who died just before her child was to be born. Her body was put into a cave, which was sealed with a stone. A plant sprouted from her navel and managed to creep out of the cave. It grew across the country until at last it reached the house of a chief, where it produced a gourd. The gourd was kept carefully wrapped in a fine *tapa* cloth until at length it broke open, exposing two seeds. In time the two seeds grew into twin

*Numbers refer to numbered entries in References, Chapter 15, pages 242–43.

girls who became the ancestors of all the people of the region.
[2]

From the Was of Indochina comes this long account:

In the beginning of time, they say, three *pappada* ("hills") were
inhabited by two beings, who were neither spirits nor human, and
who, though they seem to have been of differing sex, had no earthly
possessions. They existed spontaneously from the union of earth
and water. These the Wa call Yatawm and Yatai, while the Shans
name them Ta-hsek-khi and Ya-hsek-khi. The Creator Spirit, who
is styled Hkun Hsang Long, saw them, and reflecting that they were
well suited to become the father and mother of all sentient beings,
he named them Ta-hsang Ka-hsi ("Great All-Powerful") and Ya-
hsang Ka-hsi ("Grandmother All-Powerful"); and from his dwell-
ing-place in the empyrean, which is called Mong Hsang, he dropped
two *hwe-sampi*, or gourds, down to them.

Picking up the gourds, Yatawm and Yatai ate them and sowed
the seeds near a rock. At the end of three months and seven days
the seeds germinated and grew into large creepers; and in the course
of three years and seven months the creepers blossomed, each producing a gourd, which, by the end of the full period, had swollen
to the size of a hill. At the same time Yatawm and Yatai and the
twelve kinds of creatures (concerning whom no details whatever
are given) came to know the sexual passion. There is here a kind
of suggestion of the Tree of Knowledge of Good and Evil, but with
no hint of an assumption that Hkun Hsang Long did not intend
the gourds to be eaten. When the gourds had reached their full
size, the noise of human beings was heard inside one, and the noise
of all kinds of animals inside the other.

Ya-hsang Ka-hsi at the same time grew great with child and gave
birth to a girl who had the ears and the legs of a tiger, whence her
parents called her Nang Pyek-kha Yek-khi ("Miss Queen Phenom-
enon") and made over to her all the expanse of earth and water
and the two gourds. Apparently the eating of the first two gourds
had brought death into the world as well as passion, for the two
first beings, we are told, were now well stricken in years, so that
they called aloud and addressed the Nats and Thagyas, the spirits
and archangels, vowing that whosoever was able to split the gourds
should have their daughter to wife.

At this time there was one Hkun Hsang L'röng, who had come down from Mong Hsang in the skies and by eating the ashes of the old earth had become so gross and heavy that he lost the power to reascend to his own country. This suggests the *thalesan*, or flavoured rice, of Burmese legend, which brought about the debasement and fall of the original celestial Brahmas. Hkun Hsang L'röng was, therefore, constrained to remain upon earth and be associated with the spirits of the hills and dales, the trolls and pixies and kelpies, and he wandered far and wide. He passed through the three thousand forests of Himawunta (the Himalayas), he wandered to the foot of Loi Hsao Mong, which seems to be a Wa equivalent for Mount Meru, and he crossed mighty rivers and fells to the sources of Nam Kiu (the Irrawaddy), and thence over to the Nam Kong (the Salween), which borders the Wa country on the west. Finally he came to the place where Yatawm and Yatai lived, and when he saw their young daughter Nang Pyek-kha Yek-khi, he fell in love with her, in spite of her tiger's ears and legs, and asked for her hand in marriage. The old people were not unwilling, but they told him of the vow which they had made to the spirits of the air, and insisted that only the man who had the power to split the two gourds should wed their daughter.

Then Hkun Hsang L'röng recalled the pilgrimages which he had made and the merit that he had thereby gained for himself, and he called aloud and said: "If indeed I be a Bodhisattva who, in the fullness of time, am destined to become a Buddha and to save all rational beings, then may the Hkun Sak-ya (Indra) and the Madali Wi-hsa-kyung Nat, that powerful Spirit, descend and give me the two-handed Sakya sword, the celestial weapon!" Thereupon the two eternal beings came down from the Elysian Fields and gave him the magic falchion, two-edged and wonderful. With this he cut open the two gourds; first that which enclosed all the animals of the earth, and then that in which the human beings were contained. . . . The races of men that came out of the great gourd were sixty in number, and they were divided into four classes: those who lived on rice; those who lived on maize; those who lived on flesh; and those who lived on roots. Each had its own language and raiment and manner of living. From these are descended the five clans of Yang (Karens), two clans of Pawng (who they were does not appear), five clans of Tai (Shans), six clans who were neither Khe nor Tai, and thirteen clans of Hpilu Yek-kha. [3]

From southern India comes a story that tells us how Kwoto, also known as Meilitars, one of the gods of the Todas, came from a gourd.

There was once a man belonging to Melgars who married a woman of Kanodrs and took her to Melgars. When she became pregnant, the woman was taken by her husband to Kanodrs. On the way back to Melgars they passed Ushadr, the place where the funeral ceremonies of Melgars men took place. They were standing in front of the funeral hut at that place when the man found a good *twadri* tree, and, cutting three or four sticks from it, brought them to his wife, who stripped the bark from the sticks. While she was doing this, the pains of labour came on, and soon after she gave birth to a gourd *(kem)*. Both husband and wife were very much ashamed, and they decided to say that a child had been born and had died, and the man went round to all the villages to say that this had happened and that the funeral would be held at Ushadr. Accordingly they had the *etvainolkedr* (first funeral ceremony) at Ushadr, the gourd being covered with a *putkuli* (cloak), so that it was taken to be the body of a child.

First the buffaloes were caught and killed, and then the supposed corpse was taken to the burning-place, where a fire was made and the gourd in its mantle was put on the fire. The fire first burnt the cloak, and when it reached the gourd, this broke into two pieces. One piece became a little baby, a boy, which took a piece of the burnt cloak and went away in the air to Neikhars, where there is a big tree, under which it alighted. The other piece of the gourd was split into many fragments by the heat of the fire, and some of the fragments were driven with such force that they killed a kite which had come to the funeral. (To this day the kite does not eat the buffaloes at funerals at Ushadr, though it does so at other places.) The father and mother followed the child to Neikhars, where they found it sitting on the tree. The father and mother said to the child "Ena, itva"—"My son, come here," and the boy came down and went to them, and was taken away by his parents to Melgars. [4]

The creation myth of the Nuers of Africa has a large gourd falling from the heavens. It contained a spear, an animal's skin, and a man. The man was called Kier and he was the father of the first Nuer. A variant of this story tells us that it was Yul who found Kier. Yul was traveling with his people when a gourd fell from the skies. It was a huge gourd, bigger than a person. Yul told the people to take the gourd, but they were afraid and fled, so Yul was left alone beside the gourd. He was not afraid and split it open. Kier stepped out of one side, and the other side contained seeds. At first Kier would not go to the village with Yul, but eventually the people of the village came to him and said they had a girl for him. So Kier went to the village and had children. [5]*

According to a myth of the Apinayes of central Brazil, the supernatural creators, the sun and the moon, tossed fresh gourds into the ocean, and the gourds turned into humans. When the great flood came—a belief in a great flood is common to many cultures—some people were able to stay alive on a gourd raft, and they became the ancestors of these Indians. [6]

Another story of the origin of people from a gourd comes from the Potsawugoks of Venezuela. The name of the people is derived from their word for the drinking gourd, *potsaw.* In ancient times the people fought until there was only one man left alive. This man took a gourd and copulated with it, thereby giving rise to the people. It is said that those from Santa Elena do not know how to talk but "make gurgling noises, like people drinking out" of a gourd, for they originated in a gourd. [7]

The use of the gourd to make people wasn't always successful, as is indicated by this story from Easter Island.

Makemake looked for a calabash filled with water. He masturbated in the water of the calabash. Red flesh sprouted out. It was no good. He tried again with a stone, he masturbated with a stone. It was no good. He tried with earth. He molded and masturbated with it. There was a bad odor. Then were born Tive, Rarai, Hova, and the old woman, Arangi-kote-kote. [8]

*Many of the accounts that I am telling in my own words have been considerably condensed, but insofar as possible I have not altered the original story.

THE BOTTLE GOURD

According to a myth from the West Indies, a gourd is responsible for the bitterness of the sea.

Long, long ago, there once lived upon an island of the West Indies, a strong powerful man named Iaia, who had a single son whom he loved dearly. In those days the sea which surrounded the island was as sweet as spring water and Iaia and his son used to catch fish in the fresh water. One day the son of Iaia died and his father desired to bury him, but could find no place which was suitable so he put him in a great gourd and carried it to the foot of a high mountain. Once every noon Iaia was wont to visit the place of the gourd in order to ease his loneliness, and on one of these visits he felt an overpowering desire to see the body of his well beloved once again. This feeling grew and grew until on one of his visits he brought himself to open the great gourd which contained the body of his son. When the gourd was opened, great was his astonishment to find it full of water in which were swimming great whales and other fish of enormous size. Filled with fear at such a sight, he carefully put back the cover on the gourd and returning to the village he told his wife what he had seen, after getting her to promise that she would tell no one. This woman had a sister who had borne four boys at a single birth and the two sisters were wont to go together to the stone mill to grind the maize and at these times, as is the custom of all women, they talked. So without thinking the woman of Iaia told her sister about the gourd and the mighty fish which were swimming around in it. And the sister told her sons and they planned to take away the gourd for the fish which it contained.

After some difficulty, the four brothers found the gourd of Iaia and were loading it into a litter so as to take it home with them, when Iaia came again to visit at the tomb of his son. Terrified at the sight of Iaia, the four dropped the great gourd which fell upon a rock and split into pieces. From these holes such a quantity of water poured out that the whole earth was flooded and many people including the four brothers, their mother and Iaia's wife were drowned. At last the waters ran down into the sea and the dry land appeared once more and the village was rebuilt. But now the water of the sea was no longer fresh, but bitter tasting like the juice of a gourd. [9]

Another story from the same region, very similar to the one given above, holds that the sea itself came from a gourd. [10]

The gourd also figures prominently in myths dealing with the origin of agriculture or the pursuit of food in many places. It is told that when the ancestors of the Caingangs of Brazil suffered from the lack of food, their "chief told them to cultivate a piece of land by fastening a creeper around his neck and trailing him on the ground. Three months later his penis produced maize, his testicles beans, and his head gourds." These same people realized that the gods had given them the gourd as a rattle when they saw one on a dancing bush. [11]

The gourd is also among the first plants of the Chokwes' of northeastern Angola. When the people came from the East they could find no food, but a hunter was lucky enough to kill a bird. On opening it he found seeds of various plants. So he and his companions decided to proceed in the direction from which the bird came, and at length they found an area full of wild maize, gourds, and other edible foods. [12]*

From Togoland we learn of an old man with magical powers that enabled him to send out a gourd to search for food, which would always return filled. Among these people the gourd was a symbol of productivity. It became the magical possession of a woman after she reached puberty and was so sacred that it was buried with her. [13]

The "Prayer of the Gourd," or *Pule Ipu*, was used in Hawaii when a boy was separated from his mother and installed in the men's living quarters. A pig was offered as a sacrifice, and its head, which had a gourd suspended from the neck,

---

*It should be pointed out that maize is not native to Africa, nor to Indochina, where it was mentioned earlier. It did not become a cultivated plant in either place until after Columbus' time. Thus, there has been an error in the translation of the myth, the myth itself changed after the coming of maize, or the myth is of recent origin. The mention of a plant in a creation myth can hardly be used to determine the plant's place of origin.

was set aside for the god, and an ear of the pig was placed in the gourd. After the ceremony the child was free to travel to the end of the earth.

Arise, O Lono, eat of the sacrificial feast of awa set for you, an abundant feast for you, O Lono!

Provide, O Kea, swine and dogs in abundance! and of land a large territory—for you, O Lono!

Make propitious the cloud-omens! Make proclamation for the building of a prayer-shrine! Peaceful, transparent is the night, night sacred to the gods.

My vine-branch this, and this the fruit on my vine-branch. Thick set with fruit are the shooting branches, a plantation of gourds.

Be fruitful in the heaped up rows! fruit bitter as fishgall.

How many seeds from this gourd, pray, have been planted in this land cleared-by-fire? have been planted and flowered out in Hawaii?

Planted is this seed. It grows; it leafs; it flowers; lo! it fruits— this gourd vine.

The gourd is placed in position; a shapely gourd it is.

Plucked is the gourd, it is cut open.

The core within is cut up and emptied out.

The gourd is this great world, its cover the heavens of Kuakini.

Thrust it into the nettings! Attach to it the rainbow for a handle!

Imprison within it the jealousies, the sins, the monsters of iniquity!

Within this gourd from the cavern of Mu-a-Iku, calabash of explosive wind-squalls,—till the serene star shines down.

Make haste! lest the calabash sound, and the mountain bird utter its call!

Take hold of it and it crouches; take hold of it and it displays itself at Vavau.

It has been calm and free from disturbances into the night, O Lono, free from the turbulent enmities and bickerings of the kahunas, hunters after men.

Arrest them O Lono! arrest the malicious sea-birds of Maa-ku-newa, with their flashing wings!

Confirm this and make it sacred, wholly sacred, O Lono!

Bind it securely here! The faults will be put in the background; the babbling waters of Waioha will take a second place. [14]

A story of a sacred calabash also comes from southern Rhodesia. Mukangansii, a chief of the Vambires, had potent charms to aid him in stealing, for it was necessary to steal cattle in times of famine. His charms were kept in a calabash, which had a lid with a lock that he had bought from a Portuguese trader. His sister Chifede and a pack of dogs guarded the calabash when he was absent. A terrible famine came and after consulting his magic dice he learned that the only cattle available were in the land of his dreaded enemies, the Amandebeles, who would know that he had stolen them and would take revenge. With his magic calabash and the charms he set out with the other men to get the cattle. His charms put the cattle to sleep and he stole them. They went home and feasted on the cattle, but the next day they were surrounded by the enemy. Death would be sweet, he felt, if only he could save the sacred calabash. Mukangansii took out the charms and told his sister to hide them. The men were all killed, but the women were spared, for they would fill the need caused by the absence of the Amandebeles from their own women. Their chief got the sacred calabash and asked Chifede for the key. She gave it to him, but the calabash was empty. "Where are the charms?" he asked her. "Surely, you know, O great one," she taunted him, "that a . . . chief takes his charms into battle with him." So he searched the dead bodies, but failed to find the charms. "Search her," he told his men, but she flung herself over a precipice into a lake. They dragged the lake, recovered her body, but found no charms, for they had been taken by the Great Moon Mother. [15]

In a tale from hunters of Togoland, the gourd plays a minor but significant role. An elephant whose tail had been cut off by Kwaku wanted revenge and her tail back as well, so she changed herself into a girl and entered the village where Kwaku lived. The elephant girl was admired by all the men of the village, for she was very beautiful. The men soon learned that she was single, so they suggested that she should be married. The elephant girl said that she would marry any man who could get her calabash for her, for she had brought along a calabash which she had thrown high into a tree. The men tried, but failed to get it. Kwaku's sister, who was present, said that if her brother were awake he could get it for her. The elephant girl told her to awaken him. She did so, and Kwaku shot down the calabash with an arrow. And so they were married. But the story doesn't end here, for the elephant girl turns into an elephant again and demands her tail back, but Kwaku escapes, and on and on the story goes. [13]

The gourd figures in a similar but more prominent way in the story of the calabash cup from the Tivs of Nigeria. One day the chief was returning from bathing in a stream when he saw a calabash vine growing in a tree. High in the tree he saw a calabash that would make a perfect drinking gourd. The chief climbed the tree and with much effort reached the calabash. As he started to pull it off he was startled to hear a small voice crying out for its mother to help it. The mother vine quickly put her tendrils around her child's body and pulled it out of the chief's hands. He tried to grab it again, but the mother vine made it impossible, so, rather despondent, he climbed down the tree and returned to his village. Once there he proclaimed that anyone who could fetch the calabash for him would be rewarded with his daughter for a wife. Many strong men tried, but all failed. Finally a wrinkled old magician decided to have a go at it. It took him a long time to climb the tree, but finally he reached the calabash, and now with the use of charms he made himself invisible. Quickly he grabbed the calabash, which again called to its mother for help, but the mother, seeing no one, was not able to help the child. The magician returned to the village with the little calabash, and all the while it yelled, "Mother, help me!" At last the mother vine realized what had happened, so walking with her tendrils she came to the village. She arrived too late, for a great feast was being held and the chief was drinking beer from the calabash. When night came he placed the calabash on the pole supports of his hut. The mother vine could not reach the calabash, but she was near it. There she stayed, quite content, and produced many more children so that soon every person in the village had his own drinking gourd. [16]

In a story from the Chambalas of Africa, the gourd again talks, although what it means to say is not too clear, at least in translation. In this story we also find other elements from some of the earlier stories. One day the children of a village were playing in the fields and they saw a gourd. "The gourd is growing big," they said, and the gourd said, "Gather me, and I will gather you." At once the children ran home to tell their mother about the gourd that talked, but she, of course, didn't believe them. The older girls decided to go with the children to see the gourd, and again they said, "The gourd is growing big," but this time there was no reply from the gourd. When the children went back again by themselves, however, the gourd again said, "Gather me and I will gather you." The gourd grew until it became as big as a house and ate up all the people except for one old woman. This woman gave birth to a son, and when he had grown up he asked for his father. His mother then told him that his father had been eaten by a gourd which had gone into the sea. The young man was determined to find his father, so he went to the sea and called for the gourd to come out. Nothing happened, so he went to a second place and called again. This time the gourd came out and chased him up a tree. He called for his mother to bring his bow and arrows. He fired six arrows, and the gourd bellowed loudly and at last was dead. So the boy called for his mother to bring a knife, and when he had cut it open all of the people stepped out. When they found out who had saved them they made him the chief. [17]

From the Ekois of Nigeria comes a story in which the gourd serves as guardian of a girl. Once the slaves rebelled and decided to kill all their masters, but one of the slave girls loved her mistress and decided to warn her. The mistress, however, took no heed, and so she was killed. She left a tiny baby, which the faithful slave girl took with her. When her sweetheart told her that they must also kill the baby, the slave ran back to her mistress' house, where she left the baby.

While the babe lay alone she began to cry, and at the sound, one of the big calabashes, which hung against the wall of the room, called to her and said, "Do not weep any more." After that Calabash slid down off the wall and said to a basket and matchet which were lying near:

"Go to the farm of the child's mother and bring plantains." Both went and did as they were ordered, and when the fruit was brought home, Calabash called to a pot and said:

"Go down to the river and fetch water." This also was done. So Calabash cooked for the babe and tended her many years till she grew into a very beautiful maiden.

One day the son of Obassi Nsi went hunting in the bush. After a while he came to a ruined village, in which only one house was still standing unharmed, and from this smoke was rising. He went up to it and there saw a beautiful girl who had evidently just come out of the fatting-house. The room was empty save for herself and a great quantity of calabashes. So beautiful was she that he wished to have her for his sweetheart. She was willing, so he stayed with her for some time and then went back home.

Another day he went to visit her again and asked, "Do you live here alone, or is anyone with you?" This she would not answer. After a while he began to ask her to go with him to his father's town, but in the end had to go alone, because she was afraid to leave Calabash.

After the young man had gone, Calabash said to her fosterling, "Next time your sweetheart comes, go home with him." The girl answered, "Why should I go, and leave you alone?"

That night, the son of Obassi said to his parents, "While I was hunting I found a town in the bush, and in it one very beautiful girl dwelling alone. I married her, but she will not leave her home and come with me." His father answered, "Tomorrow I shall send my people with you to bring her hither."

Next day, the Prince set out with a great train, and when Calabash saw them coming, she said to her fosterling, "Let us go now with your husband. . . ." [18]

Another story from the same source tells of a son born to a poor couple. He comes into the world with a Juju knife in one hand and a small calabash full of Juju in the other hand— Juju defies precise description, but it can loosely be described as a mysterious force of nature that often has magic property. Later in the story, when the boy is older, we learn that the calabash of Juju made him invisible when he carried it. In still another story of these people, a magic calabash figures prominently in bringing the first water to the earth. [18]

In a rather long and involved story of "The Lion Who Took a Woman's Shape" from the Hottentots, a lion ate a young girl who had gone to gather herbs in the fields, but he took care to leave her skin intact. He put on the skin and the girl's dress and went to her home. After several adventures there, the people finally discovered that what they had thought to be their daughter was in reality a lion. So the people very cautiously put dried grass over the sleeping lion and set fire to it. As the fire raged, the heart of the girl jumped out upon the ground. The mother picked it up and placed it into a calabash. Then the mother took milk from the cows and put it into the calabash with her daughter's heart. The calabash increased in size, and as it did so the girl began to grow. One day when the mother was gone the girl came out of the calabash and cleaned up the house, telling the Hare (who had figured prominently earlier in the story) that it must tell the mother that he had done the work. The mother returned, and the Hare did as he was told. But the mother didn't believe him, and, looking into the calabash and finding it empty, she searched the house and found the daughter. They embraced and kissed, and from that day on the girl stayed with her mother. [19]

A story beginning "Once upon a time" and ending "they lived happily ever after" is from the Agikuyas of Africa. A girl who had a very cruel father was sent to bring water from the river. She found that by mistake she had brought her father's porridge calabash instead of her own water calabash. Realizing that the river water would spoil the taste of the porridge, the frightened girl lost her hold on the porridge calabash, and it was washed down the river. She chased it for hours, yelling for it to come back. At length it arrived at a place where the water was very still, and she was able to pick it up. When she looked up, many crocodiles were swimming toward her, and as she hurried away an old man saw her and asked what she was doing at this dangerous part of the river. She explained to the old man what had happened and about her cruel father, so the old man accompanied the girl to her home and explained to the father how she had risked her life to save his calabash. From that day on the father was never cruel again. [20]

The tale of the calabash children from the Chagas of Tanzania, however, does not have such a happy ending. A poor childless old woman, whose husband was dead, had to work very hard. So every day she prayed for help. One day when she was hoeing her gourds, a messenger from the Great Spirit appeared and told her that if she tended the gourds carefully she would be rewarded. When the gourds were harvested, she scooped out the pulp and put the gourds on the rafters in her hut to dry, except for one which she placed beside the fire so that it would dry more quickly. When she had gone to weed her bananas the next day, the messenger of the Great Spirit returned and changed the gourd beside the fire into a boy, Kitete, and then the messenger turned and changed the other gourds into children. After he left, the young children called to Kitete to help them down, which he did. Then all of them except Kitete, who was very lazy and foolish, began cleaning the house and hoeing the garden. After the tasks were finished, they all turned into gourds again. This happened for several days before the old woman, alerted by her neighbors, returned from the field suddenly one day to see for herself what was happening. When she found the children, she wouldn't let them turn into gourds again. She cooked for them, and they continued to work for her until she became very rich. But then one day she tripped over

Kitete, who was sleeping by the fire. This caused her to lose her temper, and she yelled at him, "You're nothing but a worthless calabash." Just then the children came in from the field, and she said to them, "Why, you're nothing but calabashes, too. I can't imagine why I cook for you." Before she could say another word, they all turned back into gourds. The woman realized what a fool she had been, but it was too late. The gourds never changed into children again, and from that time on she lived alone, getting poorer day by day until she finally died. [21]

The next four stories all concern gourds and wealth as well as mean people; the first three are from Africa and the last is from Brazil.

By a stroke of luck Wend'Yamba, an orphan, sold a scrawny chicken, his only possession, for a thousand cowries. When Piga, the mean mother of the family with whom he lived, learned of this, she became jealous and made Wend'Yamba scatter the cowries in a field. It soon rained, and the cowries disappeared under the mud. A week later the field was full of calabash plants. Piga was excited at this and ran to tell her husband that they would be rich when they sold the thousands of calabashes. But her husband knew that he had not planted any seed, and when he dug up a plant he found that it came from a cowrie. "You mean, Wend'Yamba will be rich," he told Piga. This made Piga angry, and she told Wend'Yamba to destroy the plants. "No," her husband told her, "the calabash is a symbol of prosperity and is sacred." Piga decided to wait, for she knew that, although the plant was sacred, the fruits were not. So when the calabashes were ripe she ordered Wend'Yamba to take a stick and break them all. He obediently did so, and through his tears he saw, as he broke each calabash, that instead of seeds each one of them held a thousand cowries. [22]

Two ugly women asked their husbands to find them jewels to make them beautiful. The first husband made his wife some beads of clay. The second man, however, went out into the world to search for jewels. Finally he grew tired and laid down to rest under a baobab tree. The tree told him where to find riches. He went there and met a goblin. The goblin told him that his mother would pepare a chicken for him, give him the feathers to eat, and throw away the meat, and that his father would offer him two gourds and that he must take the smaller one. He did as he was told and returned home to find the gourd filled with jewels and other riches. When the first man's wife saw the second wife with all the jewels, she crushed her clay beads and berated her husband. So he set out to find jewels for his wife. Eventually he found the goblin, but he made fun of being served feathers and was very discourteous. So the goblin didn't tell him which gourd to take, and naturally he took the larger one. When he returned home and opened the gourd, out emerged a huge cudgel which proceeded to beat him. [23]

Then there is the story of a little girl who sold palm oil in the market. Late one day a goblin bought some palm oil and paid her in cowries. He paid her one too few, and the girl cried that her mother would beat her if she went home one cowry short. The goblin walked away, and the girl followed him. "Go away," the goblin said, "for no one can follow me," but the girl did, and try as he could, the goblin could not get rid of the girl. At long last they entered the land of the dead, and the goblin gave the girl some palm nuts, saying, "Eat the palm oil and give the remains to me." But the girl gave the palm oil to the goblin and ate the remains herself. Next the goblin gave the girl a banana, saying, "Eat this banana and give the skin to me." But the girl ate the skin and gave the banana to the goblin. By and by the goblin said to the girl, "Pick three *ados* (small gourds, commonly used for storing medicinal powders), but do not pick those that say 'pick me'; instead pick those that say nothing and return to your home. When you are halfway home, break one *ado*, break another when you are nearly home, and the last when you are inside your house." The girl did as she was told. When she broke the second gourd, many sheep, goats, and chickens appeared. Then in the house she broke the last *ado*, and the house was suddenly filled with cowries. The mother took some of the things as a gift to the head wife, but instead of thanking her the head wife said that she would do the same with her own daughter. So her girl went to the market with palm oil, and sure enough the goblin appeared and bought some. He paid her the correct number of cowries, but the girl pretended that he had not and followed him. The same things happened as before, but this time the girl ate the palm oil and banana and gave the remains to the goblin. The goblin then gave her the instructions for picking the *ados*, but she did not follow his advice and picked the ones that said "pick me." Then when she was halfway home she broke open the first, and leopards, lions, hyenas, and snakes came forth and chased her. Nearing home she broke the second one, and even more ferocious animals appeared and before she could get into the house ate her up. [24]

In northern Brazil there lived two brothers: Silverio, who was rich, and Manoel, who was poor. One day Manoel went to Silverio's house to tell him that his wife and children were hungry. Silverio, pretending to be kind, gave him some land. It was worthless, but Manoel didn't know that. He was pleased, and with his wife he set out to look at the land. At last they found it, but were crestfallen to see how worthless it was. But then his wife spied a gourd; it was a golden gourd. They were very happy, for they realized how valuable it was, but Manoel decided that the gourd belonged to Silverio. They set off to tell the brother, and, after learning about it, Silverio hurried off to see the gourd, which, of course, he meant to keep for himself. However, the only thing that he could find that resembled a gourd was a huge wasp's nest. Deciding that Manoel had tricked him, he carefully put the wasp's nest in a sack and went to Manoel's house. "Open the window and I will throw the gourd to you," he said. They did so, and Silverio flung the wasp's nest through the window and waited to hear the cries as the wasps stung them. But he heard nothing, for as the wasps flew out they turned into pieces of gold. Finally, Silverio yelled for Manoel to open the door. Manoel, however, was not about to be tricked again and told his brother to go away. Only later, after he had used the gold to buy some good land, did Manoel tell his brother what had happened. The neighbors laughed at Silverio and often repeated the story of the gourd that had made a poor man rich and a rich man the subject of ridicule. [25]

A long account from the Benga tribe of West Africa involves a magic gourd that talks. The story also has the reversal of fortunes that was found in some of the stories concerning wealth, only this time the wealth is a bride instead of money. A young man, Mbuma-tyetye, decided to go out into the world to seek a wife. After many trials he met a giant tooth, who asked the young man where he was going. After the young man told him, Tooth gave him a gourd, telling him that Gourd would tell him what he must do on the remainder of the journey. Again he met many trials, but each time Gourd told him what he must do, and at length he reached a village. There he found many lovely girls, one of whom he selected for a wife, but his trials were not yet over. With Gourd's wise advice, he overcame the many obstacles. At last the chief of the village consented to the young man's taking his daughter home with him.

At daybreak, food was cooked. The Chief Njambu-ya-Mekuku, put his daughters into large chests. In one was a lame one; another, covered with skin disease; and another, with a crooked nose; and others, with other defects in other chests, each in her own chest. But, he put the wife into a poor chest all dirty outside with droppings of fowls, and human excrement, and ashes. In it also, he placed a servant and all kinds of fine clothing. Then said he to Mbuma-tyetye, "Choose which chest contains your wife."

The Gourd at once called him, and It said to him, "Lift me up!" It whispered to him, "The chest which is covered with dirt and filth, it is the one which contains your wife. Even if they say, 'Ha! ha! he has had all his trouble for nothing; he has left his wife,' do you nevertheless carry it, and go on with your journey."

He came to the spot where the chests were. The Chief said again, "Choose, from the chests, the one which contains your wife."

Mbuma-tyetye picked up the poor one. They shouted. But, he at once started on his journey, and on, until he came to the river, stepped into a canoe, paddled to the other side, landed, and went on, carrying the chest. Almost in an instant (by his magic Hgalo) he was at the place of the Great Tooth. It asked, "How is it there?" he replied, "Good!" The Gourd, in leaving, reported to Its mother, the Tooth, "A fine fellow, that person there!"

The man continued his journey, and almost in a stride he reached his home village. The chest was opened and out stepped his beautiful wife arrayed in all her finery and with a servant at her side. When the young man's brother saw the lovely girl, he immediately decided to set out to the same place for a bride. After several adventures in which his behavior left something to be desired, he encountered the giant tooth. Tooth, just as before, gave the man a gourd, telling him that Gourd would give him instructions on the rest of the journey. The man, however, didn't think Gourd could do much for him, and he constantly belittled it. He, too, went through many tests, and, reluctantly taking Gourd's advice, he finally secured a wife.

Another day broke, and his father-in-law said to him, "On the morrow will be your journey." When the next day dawned, the Chief brought out the chests containing his daughters, and said, "Now, then! Choose the one that you will take with you."
The Gourd whispered to him, "Do not take the fine-looking one; you must take the one you see covered with filth." He responded, "Not I!" The one he chose was the fine one. He took it up, and carried it away. The town's people began to cry out (in pretense), "Oh! he has taken from us that fine maiden of ours!" He was full of gladness that at last he was married. But, really, he was carrying a woman, crooked-nosed, and all of whose body was nothing but skin-disease, and pus oozing all over her.

He, of course, did not realize his mistake until he returned to his village and opened the chest. The townspeople were aghast when they saw the girl, and the children made fun of him. The brother was so angry that he changed himself into a leopard, and the hatred between mankind and leopards dates to that day. [26]

In the Chinese tale entitled "Old Man of the Gourd," we again find that the gourd has magical properties. Once in an ancient city there was an old man who was a popular street vendor of medicines and herbs. No one knew his name, so he was called the Old Man of the Gourd, because of a gourd that he hung by the wall as a symbol of his trade. A man named Fei lived on the same street, and one day, having nothing better to do, he watched the old man from his window and wondered about him. Finally after dark he saw the old man pack up his wares and, looking around to see that no one was watching, clap his hands and jump into the gourd. Fei could scarcely believe what he saw; he realized that the old man was not a mere mortal but one skilled in magic ways. So Fei decided to get to know the old man better and invited him to his house for tea. After becoming friends, Fei remarked that sometime he would like to visit the old man's home. The old man replied that indeed he must return Fei's kindness and invited him to meet him on the street at the close of the day. Fei, excited about the prospect of learning more about the mysteries of the old man, eagerly kept the appointment. When he arrived the old man put away his medicines and herbs, clapped his hands, and Fei found himself inside the gourd with the old man. What a surprise, for it was a beautiful mansion, elaborately decorated with priceless objects. "Make yourself at home," the old man said, "we have food and wine on yonder table." After the sumptuous feast with much wine, Fei remembered nothing more, and when he awoke he was in his own bed. The Old Man of the Gourd was never to be seen again. [27]

Another legend of a magic gourd also comes from China.

Sun went to meet the Demons, and in conversation learnt from them that they were on their way to catch the famous Monkey, and that the magic gourd and vase were for that purpose. They showed these treasures to him, and explained that the gourd, though small, could hold a thousand people. "That is nothing," replied Sun. "I have a gourd which can contain all the heavens." At this they marvelled greatly, and made a bargain with him, according to which he was to give them his gourd, after it had been tested as to its capacity to contain the heavens, in exchange for their precious gourd and vase. Going up to heaven, the Monkey obtained permission to extinguish the light of the sun, moon, and stars for one hour. At noon the next day there was complete darkness, and the Demons believed Sun when he stated that he had put the whole heavens into his gourd so that there could be no light. They then handed over to the Monkey their magic gourd and vase, and in exchange he gave them his false gourd. [28]

The tale of Hina-Moa and Tutanekai is a popular love story among the Maoris of New Zealand. Tutanekai and his three stepbrothers, who lived on the island of Mokoia, all fell in love with the beautiful Hina-Moa, who lived on the mainland. The three true brothers all made fun of Tutanekai, but at a dance where Tutanekai played his flute beautifully Hina-Moa was much attracted to him. Later she could hear him play his flute across the waters. When they met again a year later, they thought that they felt love for one another, but they were too shy to say anything. Finally Tutanekai sent her a note saying that he loved her, and she sent him a return note telling of her love. When he told his brothers of this, they derided him, and he decided that maybe the note didn't really come from her. Each night Hina-Moa would hear Tutanekai's flute playing, and at length decided to go to him. In the dark one night she went to the lakeside hoping to find a canoe to take her across, but there was none. She tried two other times, and still there was no canoe, but she did find six water gourds. She emptied the gourds, took off her clothes, and using the gourds as floats made her way across the lake. Just then the flute playing stopped and she didn't know which way to turn. Tutanekai had stopped playing because so much playing had made him thirsty. He sent his servant to the stream that emptied into the lake to get him a drink. Hina-

Moa heard the servant's footsteps and, disguising her voice as a man's, she asked who it was, and the man told her. As she was naked, she realized that she couldn't ask the servant to lead her to his master. So in the darkness she asked for the gourd for a drink, and she broke it. So the servant went back for another gourd. Again she asked for it and broke it. When this happened a third time, Tutanekai realized that it was being done on purpose, so he decided to go to the water and punish this unruly person. At first Hina-Moa teased him by running away from him as he approached, but eventually she allowed herself to be caught. When he grasped her hand, he realized it was a woman's. So she returned to his home with him, and shortly thereafter they were married. [29]

There apparently are very few gourd myths from North America, but one of my favorites and certainly one of the longest comes from the Senecas. A young man won a shooting contest and as a reward received the daughter of the chief. His rivals were very jealous and so arranged with sorcerers to kill him. After the wedding night the young man died. The next morning, when the saddened wife had gone to the garden to be alone, she saw her dead husband leave the house. She resolved to follow him, but she could not overtake him. After many difficulties in passing through two passageways, she reached the land of the dead, where we pick up the story.

After following the trail a long time, she finally came to a third passageway. The man who guarded it said to her: "What do you here? What brings you to this place, seeing that you are not dead?" She answered him: "I am following the trail of my husband, which leads through this passageway." Then she briefly related to him the events which had caused her to undertake the journey hither. The warder replied: "I will assist you in recovering your husband. You must take with you this gourd, which is closed with a tendon, for in this receptacle you will have to bring back the soul of your husband, carefully shut up. You must take also this small gourd bottle, which contains the fat or oil of man; you must take it with you for you will need it. When you reach a very large strawberry field stretching on both sides of the path, you must rub some of this oil on the palms of your hands."

The woman followed the instructions of the warder, and finally she came to an old woman.

The woman, who was picking berries, heard her call and stood attentive until the other woman came up to her, whereupon she said: "What do you here, seeing that you are not dead?" Answering the Mother of Ghosts, the woman said, "I come here seeking my husband, whose trail comes into this place," and so saying, she gave the two gourds to the Mother of Ghosts. The latter replied: "I will put your husband into this empty gourd bottle, so that you may take him back with you. Come then to the lodge."

The young widow followed the old woman to the lodge. When night fell, the ghosts came to the lodge for a dance. At first her husband was not among them, but at length they persuaded him to join in the dance. Some of the ghosts thought they smelled a human, but the hostess assured them that it was only she. She then tried to grab the husband of the young woman, but he eluded her grasp and all the dancers fled.

The ghosts were finally persuaded to reenter the lodge and resume the dance. Before long another opportunity presented itself, and the hostess succeeded in seizing the ghost of the newly arrived husband, while all the other ghosts escaped from the room. Quickly uncorking the gourd bottle, the hostess soon compressed the ghost therein, and securely closing it with its tendon stopper she called the embodied guest from her place of concealment and hurriedly gave her the gourd containing the husband's life, and also the small gourd which contained the oil of the body of man. Then she said to the now highly excited woman: "Be you gone now! Be quick, lest they see you; the man at the first passageway will fully instruct you what to do to have your desire fulfilled. So go."

Hurrying from the lodge into the darkness the woman followed the narrow trail. When she reached the first passageway, its warder said: "When you arrive at your home stop up with fine clay the nostrils, the ears, and every other opening or outlet of your husband's body, and then rub the oil of man over his body. When you have finished this task, carefully uncork into his mouth the gourd bottle containing his life, in such manner that his life can not escape, but will reenter his body and so reanimate it again."

The young woman made her escape and after walking for three days and nights she reached her home.

Here she quickly prepared the body of her husband as she had been directed to do, filling every opening and outlet with fine clay mixed with deer fat to soften it, and then she carefully rubbed it with the oil of man. As soon as she had completed the preliminary work she carefully and anxiously uncorked the gourd bottle containing the life of her husband into the mouth of the body thus prepared. In a few moments she was elated to see her husband's body come to life again.

This experience rendered the body of the husband invulnerable to the spells and incantations of sorcerers and wizards. The faithful wife and her resurrected husband dwelt together in peace and health and happiness until, in the fullness of years, they died and went to the land of the Mother of Ghosts. [30]

From the American Southwest comes this children's story of the "Old Coyote and the Three Gourds." These gourds could well be buffalo gourds rather than bottle gourds. A long time ago there were three gourds. One day they came out of their hole to bask. Old Coyote also came out of his hole to bask. "Let's call Old Coyote names, and if he comes after us we will flee into our hole," said the Gourds. So they started calling Old Coyote names, and he said that if they kept it up he would bite every one of them. They called him names again, and again he warned them. When they did it a third time, Old Coyote started after them. Then the Gourds fled into their hole. Old Coyote started digging, and when he reached the first Gourd, he asked, "Who was it that called me names?" The first Gourd replied, "One that is below," and, so saying, away he ran. The same thing happened when Old Coyote reached the second Gourd, and again when he reached the third Gourd. But Old Coyote kept on digging. At length he came to a stone that looked like a gourd. So he asked it, "Who was it that called me names?" The stone, being lifeless, did not answer. So Old Coyote repeated the question, and said, "If you do not answer me, I shall bite you on the spot." The angry Old Coyote bit the stone and broke all of his teeth. So that is the reason why coyotes do not bite gourds any more. [31]

Finally, we come to a song from the United States. It apparently originated in Civil War times, when a peg-legged sailor made a number of trips through the South enticing young blacks to escape to the North. The sailor would teach the song to the blacks and show them the marks left by his natural foot and the peg leg. Then he would go ahead of them and mark a trail on trees, or other objects, of a foot and a round spot to represent the peg leg. The drinking gourd in the song represents the Big Dipper; the old man, the peg-legged sailor; and the great big river, the Ohio.

> When the sun come back,
> When the firs' quail call,
> Then the time is come
> Foller the drinkin' gou'd.

> The riva's bank am a very good road,
> The dead trees show the way,
> Lef' foot, peg foot goin' on,
> Foller the drinkin' gou'd.

> The riva ends a-tween two hills,
> Foller the drinkin' gou'd;
> 'Nuther riva on the other side
> Follers the drinkin' gou'd.

THE BOTTLE GOURD

Wha the little riva
Meet the Grea' big un,
The ole man waits—
Foller the drinkin' gou'd.

Chorus:

Foller the drinkin' gou'd,
Foller the drinkin' gou'd;
For the ole man say,
"Foller the drinkin' gou'd." [32]

Appendix

Growing gourds

Although this is not intended to be a book on the culture of gourds, a few remarks on the subject may be appropriate. Most gourds are not difficult to grow, and seeds of several different kinds may be obtained from seed companies in the United States. The plants require a warm soil and should not be planted until all danger of frost is past. Generally this is about the same time as is recommended for planting sweet corn and beans. If an earlier start is desired, seeds may be planted indoors and the plants later transplanted to the garden. Great care must be exercised to disturb the roots as little as possible when transplanting, and for this reason peat or paper pots that can be placed directly into the field are recommended. The gourds all need abundant sunlight for the best growth, although they will tolerate some shade during the day. They also need a good soil and plenty of room, especially the bottle gourd, the fig-leaf gourd, and the silverseed gourd. These I generally plant fifteen feet apart in the garden. Some authorities recommend pruning, although I have found this unnecessary. It will, however, help to keep the gourds in bounds if only a small amount of space is available. Gourds may be grown directly on the ground, but better fruits will generally be secured if the plants are grown on some kind of support; if the fruit rests directly on the ground, it may become discolored and flattened on the side which touches the soil. It is sometimes impractical, if not impossible, to grow some of the larger gourds on supports. To keep the fruits from becoming lopsided, it may be necessary to move them gently to an upright position. Some of the primitive gourd planters would place a mat of dried grass or a stone under the gourd to help it preserve its shape and natural color. I have found that a small board will often serve as well.

If one is interested in growing the truly gigantic gourds, he might consider some of the ancient ways. In Hawaii a pot-bellied man was selected to plant the seeds, and he had to eat a huge meal before planting them. Then as he went to the field he stooped and held his arms as if he were carrying a huge gourd, and while planting the seeds he uttered the appropriate prayer. In New Zealand the method was simpler. The planter, with a seed in each hand, raised his arms and inscribed a huge circle so that the gourds would grow to that size. Of course, if one wants to grow a large gourd today, the first thing he should do is start with seeds from large gourds, for no amount of prayer or fertilizer will make the seed from a naturally small gourd produce a large one.

Gourds are subject to a few insect pests, and control measures may be necessary at times. Insecticides containing rotenone or pyrethrum, both of which are relatively nontoxic to humans, are usually effective in controlling the insects that attack gourds. Fungal damage is rare; but if a disease should occur, the measures used with other cucurbits, given in most any good gardening book, may be employed.

Hybridizing gourds

Making hybrids in gourds is very simple. One, of course, has to know the difference between the male and female flowers, to recognize the anthers and stigma, and to remember that with very rare exceptions it is possible to obtain hybrids only within a species. Thus, one should be able to obtain hybrids between different types of bottle gourds quite readily, but a cross between a bottle gourd and an ornamental gourd is impossible. In preparation for making the cross, a male flower of one prospective parent plant and a female flower of the other should be bagged before they open, so as not to permit the entry of insects. Glassine bags are ideal, paper sacks are satisfactory, unless it should rain, and plastic bags may sometimes be used, but they have the disadvantage of permitting a buildup of humidity within them, which may cause the flower to drop. I generally tie the bags around the flowers the day before they are to open; a little experience will enable one to recognize the proper time. As soon as the flowers have opened, the male flower is broken off and carried to the female flower, where the anthers are gently rubbed against the stigmas. The female flower is then rebagged for a day or two until the stigma is no longer receptive to pollen. If the cross is successful, a noticeable swelling of the ovary will be evident in a few days. It is a good idea to tie a small tag below the ovary so that the fruit may be readily identified later in the season. The parentage of the cross may be written on the label. The seeds then may be grown the next year, and it will be found that the hybrid will be more or less intermediate between the parents for many characters, although some of its characters may be more like that of one or the other of the parents because of genetic dominance.

Preserving gourds

Gourds to be preserved for gourdcraft or decorations should be harvested when mature or nearly mature. Perhaps the best way to determine maturity is to examine the stalk of the fruit. When it changes from green to brown or yellow, the gourd may be harvested. Even when harvested at this stage, the bottle gourds may still contain large amounts of water, so they should be put in a cool, dry place with good ventilation until they are completely dry. Some people recommend drilling small holes in the base of the gourd to hasten the drying process, but I have not found this to be particularly helpful. Some years I let my bottle gourds overwinter in the field and do not bring them in until early spring, when they are completely dry. This saves much work, for it eliminates the necessity for scraping off the molds that often form on gourds stored indoors.

Ordinarily the contents of the gourd dry up completely and there is no need to remove them. For making birdhouses, however, after the hole is bored into the gourd I usually try to remove the seeds and dried pulp. Sometimes these will shake out of the hole quite readily. At other times I have had to use a long-handled teaspoon or other instrument to remove them. A word of caution: the pulp, either wet or dry, of the bitter form of the gourd may be irritating to open cuts or sores. On two occasions, after working with such gourds when I had a cut on my finger, I found that the finger was slightly swollen and very painful the next day and that the cut took an unusually long time to heal. A friend of mine tells me that he has had the same experience and, moreover, that on opening the gourds to remove the seeds, the dust from the dried pulp was quite irritating to his nose.

Some people may also find enjoyment in doing various manipulations with bottle gourds while they are growing to produce unusual fruit. Knots may be tied in the gourd. To do so one must work with one of the slender-necked gourds, such as the dipper, and the knot must be made in the fruit when it is quite young and still limp. Young fruits may also be placed in bottles, and the fruit will assume the shape of the bottle—or so I am told. The few that I once attempted were singularly unsuccessful, for water got into the bottles and the gourds rotted. Strings may also be tied around the gourd to produce constrictions. My wife tried this, and the result was a gourd that looked like a row of sausages.

The ornamental gourds, of course, should be picked when the colors are still bright, and they may often be kept in

Gourd with simple knot. Square knots may also be made by using two gourds which are growing close to one another.

good condition for a table decoration for several months without any treatment whatsoever. Some people wax them to improve the appearance. By using a special treatment, Arlene Kunkel has found that the colors may be preserved for more than two years. One cup of 20 Mule Team Borax is dissolved in three cups of hot water. The gourds are dipped in boiling water briefly and then placed in the borax solution for fifteen minutes. They are then placed in a wire basket to dry. After several weeks, when the gourds are thoroughly dry, they are washed, dried, and polished with a paste wax.

I have no intention, nor do I have the qualifications, to discuss the use of gourds for gourdcraft, but the reader may have secured some ideas from the earlier chapters. A good account of gourdcraft is in Les Ward's *Illustrated Library of Arts and Crafts* (Fuller and Dees, 3734 Atlanta Highway, Montgomery, Alabama, 1974); but by far the best in my estimation is Carolyn Mordecai's beautifully illustrated *Gourd Craft* (Crown, New York, 1978). Additional information may be obtained from the American Gourd Society, Box 274, Mount Gilead, Ohio 43338. Some people, of course, may find it interesting to experiment on their own. All that is needed is a few gourds, a few tools, and some imagination.

References

General

Bailey, L. H. *The Garden of the Gourds*. New York, Macmillan, 1937.

Burkill, Isaac Henry. *A Dictionary of the Economic Products of the Malay Peninsula*. 2nd ed. Kuala Lumpur, Ministry of Agriculture, 1966.

Council of Scientific and Industrial Research. *The Wealth of India; a Dictionary of Indian Raw Materials and Industrial Products*. Delhi, 1948.

Dalziel, J. M. *The Useful Plants of West Tropical Africa*. London, Crown Agents, 1948.

Guppy, H. B. *Observations of a Naturalist in the Pacific Between 1896 and 1899. Plant Dispersal*, II. New York, Macmillan, 1906.

———. *Plants, Seeds, and Currents in the West Indies and Azores*. London, Williams and Norgate, 1917.

Herklots, G. A. C. *Vegetables in South-east Asia*. London, George Allen, 1972.

Organ, John. *Gourds*. Newton, Mass., Charles T. Branford, 1963.

Purseglove, J. W. *Tropical Crops. Dicotyledons 1*. New York, Wiley, 1968.

Quisumbing, Eduardo. *Medicinal Plants of the Philippines*. Manila, Department of Agriculture, 1951.

Watt, Sir George. *A Dictionary of the Economic Products of India*. London, W. H. Allen, 1889–93.

Whitaker, T. W., and G. N. Davis. *Cucurbits: Botany, Cultivation and Utilization.* New York, Interscience, 1962.

Part I. Miscellaneous Gourds

Chapter 2. Gourds of the Bible

Moldenke, Harold, and Alma L. Moldenke. *Plants of the Bible.* Waltham, Mass., Chronica Botanica, 1952.

Chapter 3. Tree Gourds

Hartman, C. V. "Le calebassier de l'Amérique tropicale *(Crescentia)* étude d'ethnobotanique," *Journal de la Société des Américanistes de Paris*, n.s., Vol. VII (1910), 131–43.

Kiddle, Lawrence B. "The Spanish Word Jicara," Tulane University Middle American Research Institute, Publication No. 11 (1944), 115–54.

McBryde, F. W. "Cultural and Historical Geography of Southwest Guatemala," Smithsonian Institution, Institute of Social Anthropology, Publication No. 4 (1945).

Morton, Julia. "The Calabash *(Crescentia cujete)* in Folk Medicine," *Economic Botany*, Vol. XXII (1968), 273–80.

Patiño, Victor Manuel. *Plantas Cultivadas y Animales Domésticos en América Equinoccial*, II. Cali, Colombia, Imprenta Departmental, 1964.

Standley, P. C., L. O. Williams, and Dorothy Nash. "Flora of Guatemala," *Fieldiana: Botany*, Vol. XXIV (1974), Pt. 10, 183–82.

Chapter 4. The Cucurbita Gourds

Bailey, L. H. "Species of *Cucurbita*," *Gentes Herbarum*, Vol. VI (1943), 267–322.

———. "Jottings in the Cucurbitas." *Gentes Herbarum*, Vol. VII (1948), 499–77.

Bean, Lowell John, and Katherine Siva Saubel. *Temalpakh.* Banning, Calif., Malki Museum Press, 1972.

Bemis, W. P., J. W. Berry, C. W. Weber, and T. W. Whitaker. "The Buffalo Gourd: A New Potential Horticultural Crop." *Horticultural Science*, Vol. XIII (1978), 235–40.

REFERENCES

Gilmore, Melvin R. *Use of Plants by the Indians of the Missouri River Region.* Washington, D.C., Government Printing Office, 1919.

Shifriss, O. "Genetics and the Origin of Bicolor Gourds," *Journal of Heredity,* Vol. XLVI (1955), 213–22.

Chapter 5. The Loofahs

Porterfield, W. M. "Loofah—the Sponge Gourd," *Economic Botany,* Vol. IX (1955), 211–23.

Chapter 6. Various Other Gourds

Wax Gourd

National Academy of Sciences. *Underexploited Tropical Plants with Promising Economic Value.* Washington, D.C., 1975.

Morton, Julia. "The Wax Gourd, a Year-Round Florida Vegetable with Unusual Keeping Quality," *Proceedings* of the Florida State Horticultural Society, Vol. LXXXIV (1971), 104–109.

Bitter Gourd

Morton, Julia. "The Balsam Pear—an Edible, Medicinal and Toxic Plant," *Economic Botany,* Vol. XXI (1967), 57–68.

Hedgehog and Teasel Gourd

Deakin, John R., G. W. Bohn, and T. W. Whitaker. "Interspecific Hybridization in *Cucumis,*" *Economic Botany,* Vol. XXV (1971), 195–211.

Part II. The Bottle Gourd

General

Best, Elsdon. *Maori Agriculture.* Bulletin No. 9, New Zealand Dominion Museum, 1925.

Dodge, Ernest S. *Gourd Growers of the South Seas*. Boston, Mass., Gourd Society of America, 1943.

Speck, Frank G. *Gourds of the Southeastern Indians*. Boston, Mass., New England Gourd Society, 1941.

Whitaker, T. W. "Lagenaria: a Pre-Columbian Cultivated Plant in the Americas," *Southwestern Journal of Anthropology*, Vol. IV (1948), 49–68.

Wilson, Eddie W. *The Gourd in Folk Literature*. Boston, Mass., Gourd Society of America, 1947.

Chapter 7. General Considerations

Cogniaux, A., and H. Harms. 1924. "Cucurbitaceae—Cucurbiteae—Cucumerinae," in A. Engler, *Das Pflanzenreich 88 Heft*. (IV: 275. II).

Davies, Oliver. "Excavations at Shongweni Cave: The Oldest Evidence to Date for Cultigens in Southern Africa," *Annals of the Natal Museum*, Vol. XXII (1975), 627–62.

Jeffrey, C. *Cucurbitaceae, in Flora of Tropical East Africa*. Edited by E. Milne Redhead and R. M. Polhill. Pt. 39–59. London, Crown Agents, 1967.

King, Hsuan. "Economic Plants of Ancient China as Mentioned in Shik Ching (Book of Poetry)," *Economic Botany*, Vol. XXVIII (1974), 391–410.

Meeuse, A. D. J. "The Cucurbitaceae of Southern Africa," *Bothalia*, Vol. VII (1962), 1–111.

Richardson, James B., III. "The Pre-Columbian Distribution of the Bottle Gourd (*Lageneria siceraria*)," *Economic Botany*, Vol. XXVI (1972), 265–73.

Sauer, Carl O. "Cultivated Plants of South and Central America," Smithsonian Institution, Bureau of American Ethnology Bulletin No. 143, Vol. VI (1950), 487–543.

Chapter 8. A Personal Note

Heiser, C. B. "Systematics and the Origin of Cultivated Plants," *Taxon*, Vol. XVIII (1969), 36–45.

———. "Variation in the Bottle Gourd." In *Tropical Forest Ecosystems in Africa and South America*, edited by Betty J. Meggers et al. Washington, D.C., Smithsonian Institution Press, 1973.

Kobiakova, J. A. "The Bottle Gourd." *Bulletin of Applied Botany, Genetics and Plant Breeding*, Vol. XXIII (1930), 475–520.

Chapter 9. Gourds Across the Ocean, I

Meggers, Betty J. "The Transpacific Origin of Meso-American Civilization," *American Anthropologist*, Vol. LXXVII (1975), 1–27.

Whitaker, T. W. "Endemism and Pre-Columbian Migration of the Bottle Gourd, *Lagenaria siceraria* (Mol.) Standley." In *Man Across the Sea*, edited by Carroll L. Riley et al., pp. 320–27. Austin, University of Texas Press, 1971.

———, and George F. Carter. "Oceanic Drift of Gourds—Experimental Observations," *American Journal of Botany*, Vol. XLI (1954), 697–700.

———, and ———. "A Note on the Longevity of Seed of *Lagenaria siceraria* (Mol.) Standl. after Floating in Sea Water," *Bulletin* of the Torrey Botanical Club, Vol. LXXXVIII (1961), 104–106.

Chapter 10. Gourds Across the Ocean, II

Lathrap, Donald W. "Gifts of the Cayman: Some Thoughts on the Subsistence Basis of Chavín." In *Variation in Anthropology*, edited by D. W. Lathrap and Jody Douglas, pp. 91–105. Urbana, Illinois Archaeological Survey, 1973.

———. "Our Father the Cayman, Our Mother the Gourd: Spinden Revisited, or a Unitary Model for the Emergence of Agriculture in the New World." In *The Origins of Agriculture*, edited by C. A. Reed, pp. 713–52. The Hague, Mouton, 1977.

Moore, Eleanor. "Gourds and the Cuna Indians," *Gourd Seed*, Vol. XXXIII (1970), June.

Chapter 11. Uses: General

Dunhill, Alfred. *The Pipe Book*. Toronto, Macmillan, 1969.

Edwards, Clinton R. "Aboriginal Watercraft on the Pacific Coast of South America," *Ibero-Americana*, Vol. XLVII (1965).

Fontinha, Mario, and Acácio Videira. "Cabaças Gravadas da Lunda," *Publ. Cult.*, No. 57 (1963), Compahnia de Diamantes de Angola.

Heyerdahl, Thor. *American Indians in the Pacific*. London, Allen and Unwin, 1952.

Hornell, James. *Water Transport.* Newton Abbot, U. K., David and Charles, 1970.

Lathrap, Donald W. "The Moist Tropics, the Arid Lands, and the Appearance of the Great Art Styles in the New World," *Special Publications*, Texas Tech University, Vol. VII (1974), 115–58.

Laufer, Berthold. *Insect-Musicians and Cricket Champions of China.* Anthropology Leaflet No. 22, Field Museum of Natural History. Chicago, 1927.

Mangelsdorf, Paul C., R. S. MacNeish, and G. R. Willey. "Origins of Agriculture in Middle America." In *Handbook of Middle American Indians*, edited by R. Wauchope, I. pp. 427–45. Austin, University of Texas Press, 1964.

Metraux, Alfred. "Indians of the Gran Chaco," Smithsonian Institution, Bureau of American Ethnology Bulletin No. 143, Vol. I (1946), 197–370.

Thompson, J. Eric S. "Canoes and Navigation of the Maya and Their Neighbors." *Journal* of the Royal Anthropological Institute, Vol. LXXIX (1949), 69–78.

Chapter 12. Uses: Penis Sheaths

Bruce, James S. *Gourd Men of New Guinea* (movie). Johnson Hunt Productions (1962).

Gell, A. F. "Penis Sheathing and Ritual Status in a West Sepik Village," *Man*, n.s., Vol. VI (1971), 165–81.

Heider, Karl G. *The Dugum Dani.* Viking Fund Publications in Anthropology, No. 49 (1970). New York, Wenner-Gren Foundation for Anthropological Research.

Heiser, C. B. "The Penis Gourd of New Guinea," *Annals* of the Association of American Geographers, Vol. LXIII (1973), 312–18.

Lam, H. J. "Fragmenta Papuana (Observations of a Naturalist in Netherlands New Guinea)," *Sargentia*, Vol. V (1945).

LeRoux, C. C. F. M. *De Bergpapoeas van Nieuw-Guinea en hun Woongebied.* Leiden, E. J. Brill, 1948.

Pospisil, L. *Kapauku Papuan Economy.* New Haven, Yale University Press, 1963.

Ucko, Peter J. "Penis Sheaths: A Comparative Study," *Proceedings* of the Royal Anthropological Institute 1969 (1970), 24–67.

REFERENCES

Chapter 13. Uses: Decorated Gourds

Bossche, Jean Vanden. "Madya, graveur de calebasses," Académie royale des sciences d'outre mer Brussels, *Mémoires*, Vol. VI (1955), Pt. 2.

Gourd Society of America. *Gourds, Their Culture and Craft.* Bridgewater, Mass., 1966.

Konan, Mildred. "Calabashes in Northern Nigeria," *Expedition*, Vol. 17 (1974), Fall number.

Menzie, Eleanor. *Hand Carved and Decorated Gourds of Peru.* Santa Monica, Calif., Karneke, 1976.

Rubin, Barbara. "Calabash Decoration in North East State, Nigeria," *African Arts*, Vol. IV (1970), No. 1.

Simpson, George Gaylord. *Attending Marvels, a Patagonian Journal.* New York, Macmillan, 1934.

Spahni, Jean-Christian. *Mates Decorados del Peru.* Lima, Peruano-Suiza, S.A., 1969.

Trowell, Margaret. *African Design.* New York, Praeger, 1966.

Villanueva, Armaro. *El Mate de Cebar.* Buenos Aires, Los Libros del Mirasol, 1962.

Chapter 14. Uses: Musical Instruments

Buckner, Alexander. *Folk Music Instruments.* New York, Crown, 1972.

Chenoweth, Vida. *The Marimbas of Guatemala.* Lexington, University of Kentucky Press, 1964.

Izikowitz, Karl G. *Musical and Other Sound Instruments of the South American Indians.* Göteborg, Elanders boktr., 1935.

Jones, A. M. *Africa and Indonesia.* Leiden, E. J. Brill, 1971.

Kirby, Percival R. *The Musical Instruments of the Native Races of South Africa.* Johannesburg, Witwatersrand University Press, 1968.

Krishnaswami, S. *Musical Instruments of India.* Boston, Crescendo, 1971.

Nketia, J. H. Kwabena. *The Music of Africa.* New York, Norton, 1974.

Roberts, Helen H. *Ancient Hawaiian Music.* Bulletin No. 29, Bernice P. Bishop Museum. Honolulu, 1926.

Sachs, Curt. *The History of Musical Instruments*. New York, Norton, 1940.

Chapter 15. The Gourd in Myth, Legend, and Fable

1. Abraham Fornander, *An Account of the Polynesian Race, Its Origins and Migrations* (London, 1878; Rutland, Vt., Tuttle, 1969).
2. E. S. Handy and E. G. Handy, *Native Planters in Old Hawaii*. (Honolulu, Bernice P. Bishop Museum, 1972).
3. Sir James George Scott, "Indo-Chinese Mythology," *The Mythology of All Races*, XII, 246–357 (Boston, Marshall Jones Company, 1918).
4. W. H. R. Rivers, *The Todas* (London, Macmillan, 1906).
5. Ray Huffman, *Nuer Customs and Folklore* (London, Cass, 1931).
6. Claude Lévi-Strauss, *From Honey to Ashes* (London, Jonathan Cape, 1973).
7. Audrey Butt Colson, "Inter-Tribal Trade in the Guiana Highlands," *Anthropologica*, No. 34 (1937).
8. Alfred Metraux, *Ethnology of Easter Island*, Bulletin No. 160, Bernice P. Bishop Museum (Honolulu, 1940).
9. Jared Kirtland Morse, *Gourd Seed*, Vol. III (June, 1942), 2.
10. Irving Rouse, "The Arawak," in *Handbook of South American Indians*, IV, pp. 507–46 (1948).
11. Alfred Metraux, "The Caingang," in Smithsonian Institution, Bureau of American Ethnology Bulletin No. 143, Vol. I (1946), 445–75.
12. Mario Fontinha and Acácio Videira, "Cabaças Gravadas da Lunda," *Publ. Cult.* No. 57 (1963), Compahnia de Diamantes de Angola.
13. A. W. Cardinall, *Tales Told in Togoland* (London, Oxford, 1931).
14. David Malo, *Hawaiian Antiquities* (Honolulu, Bernice P. Bishop Museum, 1951).
15. Greta Bloomhill, *The Sacred Drum* (Cape Town, Howard Timmins, 1960).
16. Harold Bergsma and Ruth Bergsma, *Tales Tiv Tell* (London, Oxford University Press, 1969).
17. Blaise Cendrars, *The African Saga* (New York, Payson and Clarke, 1927).

18. P. A. Talbot, *In the Shadow of the Bush* (New York and London, W. Heinemann, 1912).
19. W. H. I. Bleek, *Reynard the Fox in South Africa or Hottentot Fables and Tales* (London, Trübner, 1864).
20. Ngumbu Njururi, *Agikuya Folk Tales* (London, Oxford University Press, 1966).
21. Kathleen Arnott, *African Myths and Legends* (London, Oxford University Press, 1962).
22. Frederick Guirma, *The Tales of Mogho* (New York, Macmillan, 1971).
23. Birago Diop, *Tales of Amadou Koumba* (London, Oxford University Press, 1966).
24. A. B. Ellis, *Yoruba-Speaking Peoples of the Slave Coast of West Africa* (London, Chapman and Hall, 1894).
25. Frances Carpenter, *South American Wonder Tales* (Chicago, Follett, 1969).
26. R. H. Nassau, *Where Animals Talk: West African Folklore Tales* (Boston, R. G. Badger, 1912).
27. Lin Sian-Tek, *Folk Tales from China* (New York, John Day, 1944).
28. E. T. C. Werner, *Myths and Legends of China* (London, G. G. Harrap, 1922).
29. Erick Berry, *The Magic Banana* (New York, John Day, 1968).
30. J. N. B. Hewitt, "Seneca Fiction, Legends and Myths," Bureau of American Ethnology, *Annual Report*, Vol. XXXII (1911).
31. John P. Harrington, "Picures Children's Stories, with Texts and Songs," Bureau of American Ethnology, *Annual Report, 1925–26* (1928).
32. H. B. Parks, "Follow the Drinking Gourd," *Publications* of the Texas Folklore Society, Vol. VII (1928), 81–84.

Index

INDEX